The Hopwood Anthology

The Hopwood Anthology

Five Decades of American Poetry

Edited by

Harry Thomas and Steven Lavine

Ann Arbor

The University of Michigan Press

4/1982
am. Lit.

To the memory of Robert Hayden

Copyright © by The University of Michigan 1981
All rights reserved
Published in the United States of America by
The University of Michigan Press and simultaneously
in Rexdale, Canada, by John Wiley & Sons Canada, Limited
Manufactured in the United States of America

Library of Congress Cataloging in Publication Data
Main entry under title:

The Hopwood anthology.

"Marks the fiftieth anniversary of the Avery
Hopwood and Jule Hopwood Awards in Creative
Writing."
    1. American poetry—20th century.   2. Michigan.
University. Avery Hopwood and Jule Hopwood Prizes.
I.   Thomas, Harry, 1952–   II.   Lavine,
Steven, 1947–
PS613.H65   1981   811'.52'08   80-26111
ISBN 0-472-09328-2
ISBN 0-472-06328-6 (pbk.)

Acknowledgments

"Who Among You Knows the Essence of Garlic?" by Garrett Hongo, copyright © 1979 by *Antaeus*. Reprinted by permission.

"Walking Milwaukee" is reprinted with permission of Ashland Poetry Press from *Now, Swim*, by Harold Witt, copyright © Harold Witt 1974.

"Long Island Springs" and "The Meeting," from *Selected Poems*, by Howard Moss. Copyright © 1966, 1969, 1970, 1971, by Howard Moss. "Stars," from *Notes from the Castle*, by Howard Moss. Copyright © 1979 by Howard Moss. Reprinted by permission of Atheneum Publishers.

"Muscae Volitantes," by Lewis B. Horne, copyright © 1978 *Blue Unicorn*. Reprinted by permission of the editor of *Blue Unicorn*.

"Byron in Greece," "Face on the Daguerreotype," and "From the Provinces," from *Selected Poems*, by Norman Rosten, published by George Braziller, Inc. Copyright © 1979 Norman Rosten. Reprinted by permission of the publisher and the author.

"Flight 539," "Carmarthen Bar," and "Hotel Paradiso E Commerciale," from *The Selected Poems of John Malcolm Brinnin*, published by Little, Brown and Co., permission of the author.

"Dear Country Cousin," published in an earlier version in *Poetry Now*, copyright © 1979 by E. G. Burrows. "The Admiral's Daughter," copyright © 1980 by E. G. Burrows.

"9:00" and "Other Lives," by Patricia Hooper, copyright © 1979 the *Centennial Review*. Reprinted by permission of the author and the editor of the *Centennial Review*.

"In Place of a Curse" and "After Sunday Dinner We Uncles Snooze," from *39 Poems*, by John Ciardi, published by Rutgers University Press, copyright © John Ciardi 1959. "Minus One" and "In the Hole," from *The Little That Is All*, by John Ciardi, published by Rutgers University Press, copyright © John Ciardi 1974. Reprinted by permission of the author.

"The Day Lady Died," from *Lunch Poems*, by Frank O'Hara, published by City Lights Books. Copyright © 1964 by Frank O'Hara. Reprinted by permission of the publisher.

"The Lake: Coda," "A Difference," and "The Knot," from *When*

1979, *Seattle Review*. Reprinted by permission of the author and the editor of *Seattle Review*. "Honeysuckle" also appeared in *The Mouths of the Year*.

"When You've Been Here Long Enough," by Lawrence Joseph, copyright © 1977 *Stand*. Reprinted by permission of the editor of *Stand*.

"Ode to the Finnish Dead," from *The Unknown Dance*, by Chad Walsh, published by Abelard-Schuman. Copyright © 1964 Chad Walsh. Reprinted by permission of the author.

"Moving Day," by Lewis B. Horne, copyright © 1962 *Wascana Review*. Reprinted by permission of the editors of *Wascana Review*.

"Dream Girl," copyright © Karen Wheatley (Karen Snow) 1980. Reprinted by permission of the author.

"Saints Lose Back," "When There Were Trees," "Moss," "Bone Poem," and "Flea Circus at Tivoli," from *Carpenter of the Sun*, by Nancy Willard, published by Liveright Publishing Corporation. © 1974 Nancy Willard. Reprinted by permission of the author.

Preface

The Hopwood Anthology marks the fiftieth anniversary of the Avery Hopwood and Jule Hopwood Awards in Creative Writing. It contains poems by thirty-two recipients of the awards, ranging from early winners who have made distinguished careers for themselves to recent winners who are just beginning to publish in magazines and small-press books. Together, the poems gathered here offer a good look at some of the major directions in American poetry during the last five decades. At the same time, they honor Avery Hopwood, the founder of the awards, the teachers at the University of Michigan who fostered the writers presented here, and, above all, the poets themselves.

Since 1931, the Hopwood Awards have given encouragement and cash prizes to aspiring writers at the University of Michigan. In fact, no writing prize in America, academic or otherwise, can match the accumulated amount of the awards. They owe to the foresight and generosity of one man, Avery Hopwood, a graduate of Michigan and, from 1910 until his death in 1928, one of Broadway's most successful playwrights. In the will that left one-fifth of his estate to the university, Mr. Hopwood directed that the prizes be "awarded annually to students . . . who perform the best creative work in the fields of dramatic writing, fiction, poetry, and the essay." Further, he stipulated that "students competing for the prizes shall not be confined to academic subjects, but shall be allowed the widest possible latitude, and that the new, the unusual, and the radical shall be especially encouraged." Initially, competitions were established in the four areas set out by Mr. Hopwood and were divided between Minor Awards, open to all undergraduates, and Major Awards, open to seniors and graduate students. In 1933, the Hopwood Committee added a separate competition for freshmen, and in 1938, one for summer students. While the amount bestowed each year fluctuates, Major Awards often exceed $1,000 and have been as large as $2,500.

The size of the awards is only one aspect of their attraction. At a time when few American institutions had made a commitment to creative writing, the Hopwoods gave a focus to energies already existing at Michigan, and became an object of national interest and envy. During its early years, editors appeared at the awards ceremonies to interview new winners, and soon volumes began to be published, identified as having received the Hopwood Award. In her Hopwood Lecture (1979), Joan Didion recalled the allure the Hopwoods held for her during her student days:

> When the Hopwood Awards are mentioned I think reflexively of being an undergraduate at Berkeley and wishing Avery Hopwood had left that famous one-fifth of his estate to the University of California instead of the University of Michigan. I wanted to win a Hopwood Award. I wanted to win one not only because the very word "Hopwood" had a bigtime national sound to it, a kind of certification that the winner was on the right track, but also because the prize was money, cash, and I needed it.

Arthur Miller, attracted by that "bigtime national sound," came to Michigan to pursue his writing: "The idea of going to Michigan," he explains, "came from an acquaintance who worked in a grocery store and had been at the University for one year. The tuition was within reason, if one saved for a couple of years, but the thing that clinched it was the Hopwood Awards. . . . The idea that a University cared that much about writing made it necessary to go there."

From the start there have been those who questioned the wisdom of granting such large awards to such young writers. Partly they have been motivated by the conviction that creative writing cannot be taught. Marvin Bell has provided one answer to this objection: "Can the writing of poetry be taught? I don't know. I think it can be learned, because every good poem is an example of someone who learned how." This volume is proof, we think, that writing can be learned, and, further, that good teaching can give depth and precision to that learning. The winners themselves have testified to the continuing value of the teaching they received at Michigan. Arthur Miller has credited Professor Kenneth Rowe with helping him to "lay up standards and goals of a very private sort for a very public art." John Ciardi has praised the "great teaching" of Professor Roy Cowden, one of the first chairmen of the Hopwood Committee. Tom Clark and Lawrence Joseph have cited the generosity and rigorous practical criticism of Donald Hall. And the Hopwoods have made other forms of learning possible as well. Laurence Lieberman has acknowledged the encouragement he received from Marianne Moore, the national judge for his manuscript. For other winners it may have been such judges as John Ashbery, W. H. Auden, Ezra Pound, Wallace Stevens, Gary Snyder, Allen Tate, and James Wright. The annual Hopwood Lectures, by Louise Bogan, Saul Bellow, Malcolm Cowley, W. D. Snodgrass, Theodore Roethke, Robert Penn Warren, and others, have given the awards and writing itself a presence at the university, thereby not only recognizing individual talents but also creating an atmosphere in which writing, good writing, can occur.

In preparing this anthology, we began by asking seventy poets to submit five new poems and to suggest poems they would like to see reprinted. From these, and from our own reading and rereading of their published works, we made our selection. We have tried to keep the range of styles and subjects as open as possible. We may have overlooked poets who deserved to be included, but we feel the opposite is also true, that we have included no poets who might better have been left out.

The resources of the Hopwood Room have made our task both easier and more pleasant and we are grateful to the staff—Hilda

Bonham, Andrea Beauchamp, Maria Gouvas, and Susan Rook—for their patient assistance. We also wish to thank the Horace H. Rackham School of Graduate Studies for their financial assistance.

S. L.
H. T.

Contents

DORTHY DONNELLY

A Prospect of Swans   1
Three-Toed Sloth   3
Consider the Lilies   5
Wheels   6

BAXTER HATHAWAY

Again My Fond Circle of Doves   8
The Gorilla   9

NORMAN ROSTEN

Face on the Daguerreotype   11
From the Provinces   13
Byron in Greece   14

ROBERT HAYDEN

Those Winter Sundays   16
The Night-Blooming Cereus   17
A Plague of Starlings   19
Mourning Poem for the Queen of Sunday   20
Frederick Douglass   22

JOHN MALCOLM BRINNIN

Carmarthen Bar   23
Hotel Paradiso E Commerciale   25
Saul, Afterward, Riding East   27
Flight 539   29

KIMON FRIAR

Greek Transfiguration   32

JOHN CIARDI
In Place of a Curse   34
After Sunday Dinner We Uncles Snooze   35
Minus One   37
In the Hole   39

CHAD WALSH
Ode on a Plastic Stapes   41
Ode to the Finnish Dead   42

E. G. BURROWS
Hidden Valley   44
Dear Country Cousin   45
The Admiral's Daughter   47

HOWARD MOSS
The Meeting   48
Long Island Springs   49
Stars   52

RUTH HERSCHBERGER
Poem   57
Mulberry Street   58
Summer Mansions   59

CID CORMAN
Big Grave Creek   60
The Poppy   62
I Promessi Sposi   63
Three Tiny Songs   64

HAROLD WITT
Walking Milwaukee   65
Notre Dame Perfected by Reflection   67

ANNE STEVENSON
After her Death   68
The Dear Ladies of Cincinnati   69
North Sea off Carnoustie   71
The Mudtower   72

FRANK O'HARA
The Day Lady Died   74
Why I Am Not a Painter   75
Poem   76
Answer to Voznesensky & Evtushenko   77
A Step Away from Them   79

KAREN SNOW
Dream Girl   81

JASCHA KESSLER
A Still Life   84
Looting   85

LAURENCE LIEBERMAN
The Osprey Suicides   87

LEE GERLACH
For Peter   96
The Pilot's Walk   97
The Pilot's Day of Rest   98

MARGE PIERCY
Gracious Goodness   99
To Be of Use   100
The root canal   101

NANCY WILLARD
Moss   102
Saints Lose Back   103
The Flea Circus at Tivoli   104
Bone Poem   105
When There Were Trees   106

X. J. KENNEDY
On a Child Who Lived One Minute   108
Nude Descending a Staircase   109
Japanese Beetles   110
In a Prominent Bar in Secaucus One Day   112

LEWIS B. HORNE
Moving Day   114
Muscae Volitantes   115

PATRICIA HOOPER
Psalm   116
9:00   117
Other Lives   118

EMERY GEORGE
Homage to Edward Hopper   119
Solstice   120

TOM CLARK
The Lake: Coda   122

A Difference   123
The Knot   124

Tom McKeown
Lost in Yucatan   125
Night Clouds   126
The Graveyard Road   127

Mary Baron
For an Egyptian Boy, died c. 700 B.C.   129
Letters for the New England Dead   130

Lawrence Joseph
When You've Been Here Long Enough   132

James Paul
Everything   134
Feet, A Sermon   135
This Town   136
Honeysuckle   137

Peter Serchuk
What the Animals Said   138

Garret Hongo
Who Among You Knows the Essence of Garlic?   141
Yellow Light   143
On the Road to Paradise   145

NOTES ON THE POETS   147
NOTES ON THE EDITORS   156

Dorothy Donnelly

A PROSPECT OF SWANS

We came out through the high doors, our heads
full of Daumiers and Delacroix's, and still
elated, descended the marble steps;
and across the water a swan moved toward us,
noble, and slow as the slowest pavane.

As if she had a year and a day,
she delayed, as if she knew admirers
stood on the stair before her, that the rose
of the sunset opened behind her—alone,
illumined, afloat on an acre of lake.

And while we watched, approving the poise
and the pose, she suddenly dove, turned up-
side down like any goose, submerging
her head, like a moose after lily pads
or lily roots—a working bird

like others. Here was no opera swan,
nor emblematical, but animal,
her sinuous alabaster figure
proof enough that a thing of beauty
turns the eye, and will forever.

At an early age, with love at first sight,
seated on a hard, black, oval-backed chair
under a gas-globe light in a room
with more past than my own, I saw through the two
glass eyes of the stereopticon

my first swan, on a pond under ostrich-
tail palms, molded, so it seemed, of porcelain

or snow. That was long ago. I still
see swans, not dreamed-up like Sinbad's roc
but real as wrens. The swan is *not*

an ivory-tower type—the poets'
pet—but a bird preferred by the people.
She is everywhere: in Plato's prose,
adrift on the Avon, wan in watermarks,
flashing in neon. Though symbolists

and kings have claimed her, she refuses
to be exclusive, to be looked at only
by some presumptive royal eye,
but is visible to any idler or boy,
saunterer in parks, or gazer at the zoo.

Any day, soundless, gliding as on glass,
she may come into view on some lagoon
the green of celadon, framed
in the willow's fronds, clothed like the curved
camellia, whiter than winter's moons.

THREE-TOED SLOTH

For Patrick Boland

In the first place, the slow sloth labors
heavily under the undue derogation
of his name, the same as the seventh deadly sin,
and secondly, somewhat suffers, in our eyes,
from the dull delusion that slowness is a defect—
though we are agreed that Rome was not built in a day.

Beethoven, to name just one, knew that the slow
is neither sinful nor sad, but just a way
of moving differently and saying something else.
The sloth is not fashioned for the gigue, he is
the molto lento movement in a fugue,
the animal andante of the suite.

Though there are those who find his stone-hinged motions
laughable, he is really no comedian;
no clown, he seriously enjoys himself,
and slowly, as some play chess. His game is with gravity,
hanging all day, opposed, resisting it,
like a clam walking broadside against a wave.

Loth to leave a present place he lingers
in it exploring its riches exhaustively,
like a bee in a rose. His movements understate
sensate felicity, as, an empiricist,
he feels his way, engaged in epicurean
loitering, in an empire of space and leaves.

His languor is fabulous; he stays so still
so long that a patina appears on him
as on unrolling stones, or domes of copper;
that mossy-stump effect or lichen-look
comes from the green mask of algae that lodge
in "certain grooves or flutings" of his hair.

To one's surprise he is always reversing himself,
and he hangs beneath branches like an inverted bird,
arrested in a perpetual state of suspense.
He sleeps with his small, round, earless, octopus
head tucked safely inward, like a pearl
in a velvet pouch, at rest on his own breast.

Unlike the birds he was never intended for walking
(having no feet) yet like them was meant for the heights;
using his claws, toucan-fashion, he climbs to the tops
of tallest trees, his back to the darkness below
and, depending there in casual, catenary sag,
resembles a last year's large, disheveled nest.

He bears himself carefully, like a child carrying
a glass of water, as if from his brimming cup
he does not want to spill one drop of enjoyment.
Energy steeps in him; he is dense with sensation
as a thinker with thought, and he hangs with closed eyes
and the concentration of someone listening to music.

CONSIDER THE LILIES

When one of those lilies-to-be-considered was looked at,
regal in the unspun stuff of its swanwhite glory,
it seemed at a standstill in time, changeless, like a flower
of alabaster. Then, overnight, overtaken
by life's perpetual motion, the tip of a petal
turned brown—abrupt reminder that flesh is as grass,
marble as mortal as the petal, and that moment by moment
beauty's dismemberer, time (the prime mover), was moving
the elegant lily toward its inelegant end.

Like the wilting lily's, man's skin wrinkles and withers,
but the man within, like the palm by the running waters,
is renewed every day. Under inner sun he prospers
like the green bay tree. Hokusai, raptly capturing
a goldfish or hibiscus with his brush, thought ninety years
not enough! Oh, the mind, alive in its time-battered arbor
can flourish like the lily-of-the-field-in-its-prime, can cope
with cold like the winter rose that flowers in the snow,
counter dark clouds like the seven-tiered arch of the rainbow!

WHEELS

Wheels are works of wit: the Greek with their neat
corollas, four-petaled and formed of metal and air;
the barrow's Cyclops eye, and the spider-web circles
that twinkle on cycles, and the airy rings on gigs,
all spare compared to the Japanese coach's twin giants:
full-flowered, thirty-spoked, yellow chrysanthemum wreaths.

The early world got the wheel and it was as welcome
as camels to nomads, a comfort in this vale of friction
where it takes things lightly; a prime mover like seven
league boots, it's an ornament, too, gliding with the calm
of a swami unmindful of time or place, everywhere
with an equal grace; suavely; the swan of the streets.

It carried kings to and fro in Sumeria, Naxos,
Assyria; it was the star of the chariot era
flashing through fields with satellite lions to war;
it rolled the carts on the cobbles, the prams in the parks,
and bowled down boulevards smoothing the path for elegant
Manet ladies poised in their polished calash.

Dappling the air with a firework flaring and falling,
the wheel performs like sun on petals of glass
in a rose window, like wind exposing the silver
concealed under leaves; wheels do what fountains do
to light, pick it apart and cast it aside,
diverted, divided, and brilliantly multiplied.

Even when old and abandoned in battle or barnyards,
propped against fences, battered and scarred, they still sparkle
like the gold-leaved wreath when the victor's head has fallen;
their irrepressible rays—signals that say
we lose our vision unless we look—make all
our vertical values, so prone to collapse, stand up.

The wheel, beginning to move, moves *us* in its whirl;
we are carried away by the radiant change in the facts
as the axle turns up gold in the ore of the air
and a cloud of dust is churned to blue mosaic,
and commerce becomes a concourse of planets, distant
cousin to the floating traffic of uncrowded stars.

Baxter Hathaway

AGAIN MY FOND CIRCLE OF DOVES

Again my fond circle of doves comes to me,
My little rabbits with wings who have downed their fears

And sallied their flutterings forth on air.
That air comes bright and blueness lives on hills.
Bell season and kind vistas.
This with the touch of a hand,
A half smile on lips that would drown need in need.

Where have you voyaged all these months of pain
When even the rats have kept their holes,
When bee has not spoken to flower,
When moss has grown gray on the rock
And grass has shriveled to root-tips?
What dwarves have you met on your travels who chattered like pies
    and wore strange hats?
What did the giants want with their clubs and thumbs besides
    clomping?
I was ploughing my garden and outlasting time.
It was not a clement season.

They walk down from the blue, the little fly-rabbits.
Their eyes blink from the bright air
And light is in their wings
As they come to my shoulders.

THE GORILLA

People who came to see the great gorilla
Behind his bars at the zoological gardens
Usually thought of him as almost human,
Having come there astride the inhuman buses
Away from the eyeless faces of the city
To arboreal alleys that were falsely rural.

Then, they were predisposed to call the rural
A pastoral boredom, and the surrounding city
A troubled jungle of all things inhuman.
Comic they found the zoological gardens
And comic likewise was the great gorilla,
Innocent of fierce aggression like the buses.

But fear of use made them acknowledge buses;
That terror was themselves; and all their city
They thought comprised of deadlier zoological gardens
In which no place loomed for the merely human.
It could be mirrored better in the rural
Image of the flea-cracking, dazed gorilla.

But then the lock broke, and the black gorilla
Stalked the trim paths of the zoological gardens,
Thumbed his nose at the park's pseudo-rural
Decor, and lumbered into the streets of the city,
Panicking folk to safety in their buses,
The upholstery of which seemed suddenly human.

But though the great beast tried to appear human
Like a hayseed who comes to visit the city
And hopes to abandon hastily his rural
Absence of manners, the good folk in the buses
Angrily disowned their love for the gorilla
And fled dismayed from all zoological gardens.

Now no one travelled to the zoological gardens
For the mirrored image of the quaintly human,
While through the streets the crazed and lonely gorilla
Stalked his loves in the escaping buses.
Since the beast had turned brick order to a rural
Landscape, people were hungry for their city.

Perhaps in time the human tribe can claim its city
When the gorilla is caught and is once more rural
And buses charge to the zoological gardens.

Norman Rosten

FACE ON THE DAGUERREOTYPE

For Walt Whitman

In the beginning, we had to deny you.
Cities of whores and builders, we had no time
For your prophecies. Your light blinded us.
We hid our nakedness, pursued money.

Now you are more alien to us than ever,
With your haunted face and rather foolish stance,
And those catalogues of names and occupations
Growing over your pages like weeds.

Lord, how you exaggerate, your embrace
Drowning us in the milk of human virility.
Men, women, animals, stones, trees—
You anoint all with your seminal bragging.

In a way, you've been destructive,
Forever tying us to objects and geography,
Whereas poetry, to survive, must somehow cut free,
Blossom in a timeless air.

The truth is, I tell myself, we've outgrown you
As an older athlete his once powerful stride.
The younger men are clever, all turned pro,
With an eye not on beauty but getting ahead.

After all is said, and you put publicly in place,
Publicly unsolved, I am moved to a secret reverence.
I see your largeness, our own diminution,
Our people, generals, explorers, poets;

How small in prophecy, how big in wars—
And I see you plain, though flickering,
And finally accept you, blowzy and barnacled,
With your one-stringed instrument, our desperate glory.

FROM THE PROVINCES

FOR ALFRED LEVINSON

I'm touched that you, my one disciple,
bring me your purest meditation.
You speak lately of doubts and terrors,
your letters seem to hint of flight.
Having followed my proverbs and poverty,
you ask, What's the word from the wilderness?
You may have heard they've written me off
as an agitator who spurned the cross
in favor of lyric poetry.
                              Beware
of Jews and Romans both, their wars
and betrayals. I promise nothing.
You may or may not get a fair trial.
In politics nothing is certain.
There are some for whom Crucifixion
is a balm, they enjoy headlines.
Others prefer to remain carpenters.

What can I advise? Stay in Galilee.
Jerusalem is full of thieves.
I asked Joseph, my Sanhedrin contact,
Is this whole adventure necessary?
He said I had to go through with it,
the people were ready. Was I a coward?
Such accusations! All I needed
were a few miracles, some luck,
he argued, but all the same I vanished.
Another joker took my place,
unenvied, despite his great courage.
His resurrection hasn't changed a thing.

Stay with the Word if it suits your skill
as it does mine.
                      Write me if you wish—
Expect nothing but advice on metrics.

BYRON IN GREECE

I was a fool to come here.
Byron to Countess Guiccioli
from Greece, October 7, 1823

You would know, dear one,
having seen my crippled foot,
my savage tears, my exhaustion.
Those days in Venice, in your arms,
were all I needed, and need now.
But Europe seemed to have willed me
to this swamp-infested lowland
where Sappho, had she sung,
would have perished.

I'm surrounded by brigands and fools
devouring money (including my own)
in stupid wars. Did I say thieves?
Add that too. Freedom's possible,
the path is thorny, and I'm here
as a figure, a force supplied
by poetry—or so the rumor goes.
Poetry and gold, dear heart,
still rule the world. I bring
both, seemingly, and battle plans
which work only in favorable weather.

Lord Byron leading the peasantry!
Well, it's the penalty for passion.
Freedom's a net that's cast
too far into a future
for any to guess at the catch.
I can't, or shouldn't complain.
I volunteered to help the cause
but can't wait to kiss your breasts
in our gondola under the stars.

Will we yet have that reunion?
Your love's not peace, yet
I'd rather that chaos than
the divine serenity of angels.
Please don't destroy my poem!
Those Cantos are my link to home.
I must complete my rascally Don Juan
despite your opposition—why?
Poetry's my toy, my serious diversion
amid man's stupidities.
Leave me that necromancy.
I mean to escape this age—
Don Juan a balloon to future skies!
I can't be rapturous as Shelley;
his drowning still leaves me shaken.
And Keats taunts me with his power
while I drift, loosed to the sea,
caught on this harsh Grecian coast.

Nothing to do but wait events.
Once in the soup, learn to simmer.
I may yet return alive.
If not—a stray bullet may need
a poet's flesh—write to my publisher
in London, and make my end heroic.
He'll use it to boost the sales.

What more to say? It's night.
The sky is murky, my heart muffled.
The candle brings the damned flies
whose bite will often kill a man.
It's a hell, which would be heaven,
were my Countess at my side,
the world in darkness, we in light.
Let freedom's storm lift stones,
lift trees: we'll be warm,
with blessed sleep as victory.

Robert Hayden

THOSE WINTER SUNDAYS

Sundays too my father got up early
and put his clothes on in the blueblack cold,
then with cracked hands that ached
from labor in the weekday weather made
banked fires blaze. No one ever thanked him.

I'd wake and hear the cold splintering, breaking.
When the rooms were warm, he'd call,
and slowly I would rise and dress,
fearing the chronic angers of that house,

Speaking indifferently to him,
who had driven out the cold
and polished my good shoes as well.
What did I know, what did I know
of love's austere and lonely offices?

THE NIGHT-BLOOMING CEREUS

And so for nights
we waited, hoping to see
the heavy bud
    break into flower.

On its neck-like tube
hooking down from the edge
of the leaf-branch
    nearly to the floor,

the bud packed
tight with its miracle swayed
stiffly on breaths
    of air, moved

as though impelled
by stirrings within itself.
It repelled as much
    as it fascinated me

sometimes—snake,
eyeless bird head,
beak that would gape
    with grotesque life-squawk.

But you, my dear,
conceded less to the bizarre
than to the imminence
    of bloom. Yet we agreed

we ought
to celebrate the blossom,
paint ourselves, dance
    in honor of

        archaic mysteries
when it appeared. Meanwhile
we waited, aware
        of rigorous design.

        Backster's
polygraph, I thought,
would have shown
        (as clearly as it had

        a philodendron's
fear) tribal sentience
in the cactus, focused
        energy of will.

        That belling of
tropic perfume—that
signalling
        not meant for us;

        the darkness
cloyed with summoning
fragrance. We dropped
        trivial tasks

        and marvelling
beheld at last the achieved
flower. Its moonlight
        petals were

        still unfold-
ing, the spike fringe of the outer
perianth recessing
        as we watched.

A PLAGUE OF STARLINGS

Fisk Campus

Evenings I hear
the workmen fire
into the stiff
magnolia leaves,
routing the starlings
gathered noisy and
befouling there.

Their scissoring
terror like glass
coins spilling breaking
the birds explode
into mica sky
raggedly fall
to ground rigid
in clench of cold.

The spared return,
when the guns are through,
to the spoiled trees
like choiceless poor
to a dangerous
dwelling place,
chitter and quarrel
in the piercing dark
above the killed.

MOURNING POEM FOR
THE QUEEN OF SUNDAY

Lord's lost Him His mockingbird,
His fancy warbler;
Satan sweet-talked her,
four bullets hushed her.
Who would have thought
she'd end that way?

Four bullets hushed her. And the world a-clang with evil.
Who's going to make old hardened sinner men tremble now
and the righteous rock?
Oh who and oh who will sing Jesus down
to help with struggling and doing without and being colored
all through blue Monday?
Till way next Sunday?

All those angels
in their cretonne clouds and finery
the true believer saw
when she rared back her head and sang,
all those angels are surely weeping.
Who would have thought
She'd end that way?

Four holes in her heart. The gold works wrecked.
But she looks so natural in her big bronze coffin
among the Broken Hearts and Gates-Ajar,
it's as if any moment she'd lift her head
from its pillow of chill gardenias
and turn this quiet into shouting Sunday
and make folks forget what she did on Monday.

Oh, Satan sweet-talked her,
and four bullets hushed her.

Lord's lost Him His diva,
His fancy warbler's gone.
Who would have thought,
who would have thought she'd end that way?

FREDERICK DOUGLASS

When it is finally ours, this freedom, this liberty, this beautiful
and terrible thing, needful to man as air,
usable as earth; when it belongs at last to all,
when it is truly instinct, brain matter, diastole, systole,
reflex action; when it is finally won; when it is more
than the gaudy mumbo jumbo of politicians:
this man, this Douglass, this former slave, this Negro
beaten to his knees, exiled, visioning a world
where none is lonely, none hunted, alien,
this man, superb in love and logic, this man
shall be remembered. Oh, not with statues' rhetoric,
not with legends and poems and wreaths of bronze alone,
but with the lives grown out of his life, the lives
fleshing his dream of the beautiful, needful thing.

John Malcolm Brinnin

CARMARTHEN BAR

Hung between stretched wings, the sea bird sat—
A shape of pain—not far from where we walked
In heavy light from off Carmarthen Bar.
"Mad Christ," I said, "Christ of the cormorants,"
But you interpreted him differently—
"He thinks that's what a cormorant *should* do,
Nobody ever told him otherwise."
All morning and all afternoon, we ached
To see his Satan-pointed shoulders make
A shrinking crucifix on the wet sand.

Perhaps, had we had more to do than climb
Sir John's Hill for the seaward view, or read
Half-finished verses in the summerhouse,
We should have heard his limp cry less, or less
Insistently. But, as it was, with words
Falling and rain falling and a drum
Nobody heard, the bird's predicament—
Was he a god in whose reach, uttermost
And pitiable, only himself was caught?—
Embroiled us when we had least heart for it.

That night within Laugharne Castle when the moon's
Seagoing trumpet blew out half the stars,
And field mice whimpered, and a chuckling owl
Cartwheeled above us in the roofless light,
The human darkness of eight hundred years
Bled from a cry. It was the cormorant.
As if, by speech, we might still overtake
A mystery we could not escape, I said,
"Sweet Christus of the cormorants outstretched,"
And you said, "Bloody bird," and nudged me home.

By morning our old albatross was gone.
Did the tides take him, sprawled on his black rack?
Or was he mustered upward, his dead wings
Beating toward immolation ceaselessly?
The angel in him, or the idiot,
Had driven us away. Yet when I cried,
"Christ Cormorant, that you might scavenge me!"
Without reflection you looked down to find
His black cross posted in that shining sand.
Together then we smiled, and walked inland.

HOTEL PARADISO E COMMERCIALE

Another hill town:
another dry Cinzano in the sun.
I couldn't sleep in that enormous echo—
silence and water music, sickly street lamps
neither on nor off—a night
of islands and forgotten languages.

Yet morning, marvellously frank, comes up
with bells, with loaves, with letters
distributed like gifts. I watch a fat priest
spouting grape seeds, a family weeping
in the fumes of a departing bus.

This place is nowhere
except on the map. Wheels spin the sun,
with a white clatter shutters are shut to,
umbrellas bloom in striped and sudden groves.
The day's away, impossibly the same,
and only minutes are at all important—
if women by a wall,
a lean dog, and a cheerful humpback
selling gum and ball-points
are important. My glass is empty.
It is Wednesday. It is not going to rain.

Observation
without speculation. How soon
the eye craves what it cannot see,
goes limpid, glazed, unanswerable,
lights on a pigeon walking in a circle,
hangs on a random shadow,
would rather sleep.

How old am I?
What's missing here? What do these people

feed on, that won't feed on them? This town
needs scrolls, celestial delegations,
a swoon of virgins, apostles in apple green,
a landscape riding on a holy shoulder.

The morning stays.
As though I kept an old appointment,
I start by the cats' corridors (Banco di Roma,
wineshops, gorgeous butcheries)
toward some mild angel of annunciation—
upstairs, most likely, badly lit,
speaking in rivets on a band of gold.

Praise God, this town keeps one
unheard-of masterpiece to justify
a million ordinary mornings
and pardon this one.

SAUL, AFTERWARD, RIDING EAST

For Gerald Fitzgerald

Still a bit dazed,
I study out the sequence—what
diverting cast of eye,
what random cocking of an ear,
could with such fell abruptness
bounce & so dishevel me? Was it
that fellow in the stinking fleece,
the black figs of his nipples bared,
who watched me drop like a drugged bee?
Those sullen beauties, broad as crabs,
bent to their lettuces & cress? The icy
chuckle of the spring
that rinsed their dragging purples
& vermilions? The two
blue mountains that were always there?

Today is yesterday: my hand,
all by itself, salutes
a door that closes,
or will close.

Hearing a voice (I did hear a voice),
but seeing no man (I saw no man),
I have listened to brass,
accepted any cupful, put on the eunuch's
fastening of silk, rolled over—
a good dog. No wonder
my old road is dark.

Still, the small flowers eat my dust.
Somehow, I wait upon the man I was—
of a commission & a large address,
of rectitude & ample documents.

I think my bones are melting. The reins
keep sliding from my hands.
I jog like a baby, loved.

Courage,
my bruises whisper: you are,
at worst, the subject of a rustic anecdote.
You would not come so far to disappear.
And yet,
this breath that takes my breath away ...
What wilt thou, Lord, *have me to do?*

I feel the low sun pushing me to sleep.
Along the walls of these colossal shadows,
light like a rumor runs its fluted scales.
Nothing I see is visible.
Damascus! Damascus!

FLIGHT 539

The same March sun that polishes St. Paul's
brightens the arches of my rack of toast.
I am flying, after breakfast, to North America.
I crack my egg with an egg-spoon; it is almost

time. I yank at straps, count money and check out,
saluted by a doorman with a calfskin face
who carries one fawn glove and wears the other.
I'm glum but genial; he's aloof. He knows his place

and clearly indicates I should know mine.
London that shone at my descent with brass
militia, geraniums, throngs of happy subjects
acting naturally, now lets me pass

as though I'd packed up and left yesterday.
"Never hinder a traveler," it says, "never detain
a guest." Its thin smile reaches to the airport.
I am not happy until I see my plane,

grasshopper-still, in fog that crowds like sleep
outside the waiting room. There is "a slight delay."
I buy five-fifths of White Horse and a Penguin
Classic that I should have read and, squared away,

slump in a wicker chair. Nothing happens
for hours. I watch a covey of white nuns who gaily
chirp toward their oblivion in Africa,
a delegation handing roses to a swart Israeli

who weeps and smiles, important in blue serge.
Do they know, I wonder, just where they belong?
My passport photo, smirking, looks me in the eye.
Loudspeakers call my number: I must go along

with all my flight companions to Gate 9.
Two by two, bellwethered by a china doll,
we file out, mount the ramp, take one last look around,
and find our seats to music piped through a wall

of leatherette. We have all done this before: we're bored
and terrified. Full tilt, our backbones braced
by gravity, we run wide open, lift,
punch through a wadding cloud and, clear at last,

track a bent circle over dunes and troughs,
riding a blue ecliptic toward the Hebrides.
The monitory lights go off, we drop our belts
and sit, heads back, alike as effigies.

Five hours that I fattened on in coming over
drop off at once. I know the time, but what time is it?
I light a cigarette off Scotland and crush the butt
some eighty miles at sea. The pilot says it

's cold in Boston, that turbulence off Newfoundland
won't reach us since we're six miles up and will soon
go up to seven. I scan the dome of the known world,
trying to imagine what I see. I'd like someone

to talk to. So would the man behind me.
We stand, stretch out, yawning like old familiars,
unembarrassed, going home. He's been
in Asia Minor where, he says, "our" failures

are conspicuous. Pleased to worry this old bone,
we share our guilt like men of the same kidney.
Then, bumped apart, we sink through clouds which,
we are told almost at once, are over Sydney,

Nova Scotia. We shake hands and, separately, sit down,
having just parted forever. The coast line filters through—

a ragged lace of ice on the North Shore. Then it's
Nahant, Revere Beach smudged with drifts of snow

that look left over from an age of ice.
Leveling, we come down fast and, drifting slightly
(a gull goes by like wreckage from a blast)
in a fan of sun, are thumped to earth as lightly

as an apple from a bough. Is it still two o'clock?
I'm stretched among northern lights! I'm lost on
a reef surrounded by dim bubbles! "Ladies and gentlemen,"
the stewardess says, "we have landed in Boston."

Kimon Friar

GREEK TRANSFIGURATION

In this Aegean island of white fire
the seas flash with hot brilliance, the waves
eat into the corroded beaches of the bay.

The houses are white in the sun, the cobbled lanes
whitewashed where silly sheep stumble with bells
and black goats drop their black merd in the alleys.

The goatherd's asleep in the vineyard under the fig-tree,
the world is asleep. And I, half-sleeping, sit
on the baked terrace of this hotel over the bay,

dazed in a white flood of fire, wrecked,
on the blurred shore of memory abandoned;
by my side, the cement anti-aircraft enclosure

left by the Germans, now scratched and defiled by hens
and the occasional lizard, hung with the day's washing;
before me hard bread and cheese, a few grapes,

and a sweet white wine staining the tablecloth;
beyond, the bird cries of children as they plunge
like gulls from the hot rocks into the tepid water;

and further, along the deserted esplanade,
its empty coffee-tables and blank arcades,
the village idiot comes, stumbling and halting.

With his right hand he pulls his trousers up
that fall to his knees and trip and entangle him
over and over again; with his left hand he stoops

to gather, in some old newspapers of last night's
public announcements of our private guilt,
the steaming excrement he dropped and drops in the sun,

his mother behind him following, wringing her hands,
calling on the sweet Christ child to exact no sin
of her for this befoulment of the soul's image.

But he, apart, mumbling and stumbling proceeds,
dropping and picking up his soft golden treasure,
his coinage, his artifact, his private and personal poem.

And were I suddenly to rise out of this trance
compounded of the sun's white fire and the sea's brilliance
and my own and the world's wrack, and take it away

from him, and cast it where it belongs, on the dump
with maggots and rot, the sheeps' and the goats' leavings,
(by which the stony soil of Greece is ever sweetened)

he would weep, I know, as once he wept as a child
trailing into his mother's parlor the salty seaweed,
bits of broken colored glass, pebbles and seashell,

and she snatched them away and cast them with the garbage,
and he was taught to know the difference between good and evil.
But I am entrapped and entranced in a bright white light

through which the human cries of seagulls swim,
and he is a child skinning his knees on the rocks,
seeking that pebble that does not fade in the sun

but strangely glows with the sea's transfiguration.
And I am dazed with fear in this blind light
that is the darkness of a farther shore

from which I hear the faint sweet cries of love
like drifting foam upon the endless sea's
indifferent and listless sursurration.

John Ciardi

IN PLACE OF A CURSE

At the next vacancy for God, if I am elected,
I shall forgive last the delicately wounded
who, having been slugged no harder than anyone else,
never got up again, neither to fight back,
nor to finger their jaws in painful admiration.

They who are wholly broken, and they in whom
mercy is understanding, I shall embrace at once
and lead to pillows in heaven. But they who are
the meek by trade, baiting the best of their betters
with the extortions of a mock-helplessness

I shall take last to love, and never wholly.
Let them all into Heaven—I abolish Hell—
but let it be read over them as they enter:
"Beware the calculations of the meek, who gambled nothing,
gave nothing, and could never receive enough."

AFTER SUNDAY DINNER
WE UNCLES SNOOZE

Banana-stuffed, the ape behind the brain
scratches his crotch in nature and lies back,
one arm across his eyes, one on his belly.
Thanksgiving afternoon in Africa,
the jungle couches heaped with hairy uncles
between a belch and a snore. All's well that yawns.

Seas in the belly lap a high tide home.
A kind of breathing flip-flop, all arrival,
souses the world full in the sog of time,
lifting slopped apes and uncles from their couches
for the long drift of self to self. Goodbye:
I'm off to idiot heaven in a drowse.

This is a man. This blubbermouth at air
sucking its flaps of breath, grimacing, blowing,
rasping, whistling. Walked through by a zoo
of his own reveries, he changes to it.
His palm's huge dabble over his broken face
rubs out the carnivores. His pixie pout

diddles a butterfly across his lip.
His yeasty smile drools Edens at a spring
where girls from Bali, kneeling to their bath,
cup palms of golden water to their breasts.
His lower lip thrusts back the angry chiefs:
he snarls and clicks his teeth: "Stand back, by God!"

And so, by God, they do, while he descends
to rape those knobs of glory with a sigh,
then clouds, surceased, and drifts away or melts
into another weather of himself
where only a drowned mumble far away
sounds in his throat the frog-pond under time.

O apes and hairy uncles of us all,
I hear the gibberish of a mother tongue
inside this throat. (A prattle from the sea.
A hum in the locked egg. A blather of bloods.)
O angels and attendants past the world,
what shall the sleeps of heaven dream but time?

MINUS ONE

Of seven sparrows on a country wire
   and off in the instant ruffle
of hawk shadow, one was no flyer,
   or not enough, or was lost in the shuffle,
six stunted their little panics one spin
   around a pasture and an oak, and spun
back to whatever they had been
   in much the same row minus one.

   Is there a kismet
the size of one of seven
   sparrows? Is it
written before heaven,
   swami, in the mystic
     billion ungiven
Names? Is there a loving statistic
   we are motes of?
Whatever remembers us, finally, is enough.
If anything remembers, something is love.

Meanwhile a shadow comes to a point,
   to beak and talons. Seven surprises
start and one stops. Six joint
   excursions circle a crisis
they return forgetting. And what am I
   remembering? It was not on me
the shadow dove. I can sit by
   noting statistically.

   Is there an average
the size of one? of any?
   Is there no rage
against numbers? Of many
   motes, mathematician,
     shall none be

more than decided? for once its own decision?
          I have spun loose
again and again with your sparrows, father, and whose
hawk is this now? unchosen? come to choose?

IN THE HOLE

I had time and a shovel. I began to dig.
There is always something a man can use a hole for.
Everyone on the street stopped by. My neighbors
are purposeful about the holes in their lives.
All of them wanted to know what mine was *for*.

Briggs asked me at ten when it was for the smell
of new-turned sod. Ponti asked at eleven
when it was for the sweat I was working up.
Billy LaDue came by from school at one
when it was for the fishing worms he harvested.

My wife sniffed in from the Protestant ethic at four
when the hole was for finding out if I could make
a yard an hour. A little after five
a squad car stopped and Brewster Diffenbach,
pink and ridiculous in his policeman suit,

asked if I had a building permit. I told him
to run along till he saw me building something.
He told me I wasn't being cooperative.
I thanked him for noticing and invited him
to try holding his breath till he saw me change.

I ate dinner sitting on its edge. My wife
sniffed it out to me and sniffed away.
She has her ways but qualifies—how shall I say?—
alternatively. I'd make it up to her later.
At the moment I had caught the rhythm of digging.

I rigged lights and went on with it. It smelled
like the cellar of the dew factory. Astonishing
how much sky good soil swallows. By ten-thirty
I was thinking of making a bed of boughs at the bottom
and sleeping there. I think I might have wakened

as whatever I had really meant to be once.
I could have slept that close to it. But my wife
came out to say nothing whatever, so I showered
and slept at her side after making it up to her
as best I could, and not at all bad either.

By morning the hole had shut. It had even
sodded itself over. I suspect my neighbors.
I suspect Diffenbach and law and order.
I suspect most purposes and everyone's
forever insistence I keep mine explainable.

I wish now I had slept in my hole when I had it.
I would have made it up to my wife later.
Had I climbed out as I had meant to be—
really meant to be—I might have really
made it up to her. I might have unsniffed her

clear back to dew line, back to how it was
when the earth opened by itself and we
were bared roots. —Well, I'd had the exercise.
God knows I needed it and the ache after
to sing my body to sleep where I remembered.

And there *was* a purpose. This is my last house.
If all goes well, it's here I mean to die.
I want to know what's under it. One foot more
might have hit stone and stopped me, but I doubt it.
Sand from an old sea bottom is more likely

Or my fossil father. Or a mud rosary.
Or the eyes of the dog I buried south of Jerusalem
to hide its bones from the Romans. Purpose
is what a man uncovers by digging for it.
Damn my neighbors. Damn Brewster Diffenbach.

Chad Walsh

ODE ON A PLASTIC STAPES

FOR DR. RUFUS C. MORROW, SURGEON

What God hath joined together man has put
Asunder. The stapes of my middle ear
Rests in some surgical kitchen midden.
Good riddance to an otosclerotic pest.
And welcome to the vibrant plastic guest
That shivers at each noise to let me hear.

What would the theologians make of this?
The bone God gave me petered out and failed.
But God made people, too. One of them sawed
A dead bone off and put a new one in.
I hear now through a storebought plastic pin.
Where God's hand shook, his creature's skill availed.

Dig where they bury me and you will find
A skeleton of bone perfected in plastic.
Gleam down the buried years, synthetic bone,
Await the judgment of the Resurrection.
The shining glory or the sharp correction
When calendars and clocks read chiliastic.

Will my old stapes rise, expel my plastic?
Do I own or do I merely borrow?
God is no divorce court judge. What man
Hath joined together, he will not put asunder.
Praise God who made the man who wrought this wonder,
Praise God, give thanks tomorrow and tomorrow.

ODE TO THE FINNISH DEAD

At Hietaniemi Heroes'
Cemetery, Helsinki

In the soft Finnish summer they become
Briefly acres of roses. One hardly sees
The standard stones with name and date and rank,
Nor would a slow addition make the sum
Of all who have their rights here. The very walls
Are eloquent with names that other trees
And flowers hold in trust, who stood and sank
To earth as the gold of a birch tree falls.

There were no roses blooming when they flowered
In winter beauty. Their garden was a dim
Disorder of the frozen lakes, and firs
Lifting with snow. And some the night devoured,
And some the darkness of the crouching east,
Folded petals at the west's·utter rim,
Faithful in death against the idolaters
And the stone icons of their blinded beast.

In their far northern tongue they had a name
For Marathon; they held Thermopylae;
No traitor could be bought to sell the way.
Suomussalmi, Tolvajärvi became
The rolling syllables Pheidippides
Spoke dying to the Athens that was free.
Thou stranger, pause, and in Helsinki say
We kept her laws amid these witness trees.

"Remember the Finns," intoned the hierophants
In triple invocation to the beast,
And to the west it turned its sightless eyes.
From reddened squares the univocal chants
Of nameless choirs came to its ears with words
Of antiphon. And when their voices ceased,

It rose by jerks, as wooden puppets rise,
And twittered like a tree of maddened birds.

Walk here amid the superficial beauty
Of roses sprung from loveliness beneath.
Here is renewal of our tattered speech.
Dulce et decorum and honest *duty*
Shine innocent in silver, gold, and red;
A goodness brightens in the word of *death*.
Bloom in the beauty of your giving, each
By each, in mankind's heart, brave Finnish dead.

E. G. Burrows

HIDDEN VALLEY

Where the plow turned back,
the sumac heads hang burned out.
The land slumps to a pond
with tame swans and a split
log planed slick for a park bench.

Birch mend the failed farm slope
with white scar tissue
except for the dinosaur bones,
the ribs of an abandoned harrow unhitched
when this homestead was broken
over the knee of bare bedrock.

The woman I love is feeding swans
at the foot of the garden of red
raspberries and burdock. I hurry down
afraid she will have torn
more bread than her body can bear
or sailed off on the broad back of a swan.

DEAR COUNTRY COUSIN

Houseboats of brass
and basswood, fringed like surreys,
pass to my left,
stately in the air currents
only five hundred feet up.
Gentlemen keep
one gloved hand on the tiller
and tip their hats to the utmost.

Their ladies,
poised motionless, arranged
in wide skirts, may already
have slipped out of their masks
and droll shapes
to porpoise in a boat's wake.

Once to the west
an entire train flew over.

The air is so busy here
where I live back of the gasworks
and the experimental carriage
and aircraft factory.
Iron balloons skip
and buck through the sky,
tails heavy with magnets to catch
their loose freight downwind.

You think I have dreamed this,
but you have never been to the city.

I must watch for the express.
Occasionally it collides
for all its lights and lookouts
with a factory stack.

There is no crash. The bricks
fall like snowflakes, the chimney
dissolves with a sigh.
Patience! Give us time.
After the dirigible comes the cow.

THE ADMIRAL'S DAUGHTER

The grandfather I never knew
wore dress blues and a cock hat with plumes.
He was high up in his Lodge.
I thought he would shout "Mr. Christian!"
or rock on his quarterdeck like John Paul Jones,
but he was dead
and his photograph slumped
among the ladyfingers at his wake
in the dusty parlor in Albany.

Upstairs, the warped floors tilted
like those of a warship,
and each cramped room lay open
for inspection, its beds made
with bolster and patch quilt puffed
to erase any mark of love or illness.

On one wall I discovered
the picture of a girl in white, with white
shoes, and a bow in her hair.
My mother never said
how young she had once been
or what tales the old sea dog brought back
when he came sailing home of a Saturday.

I doubt if he knew her any better than I did,
his eye like mine
fixed through the long glass on those chiefs
he might dazzle with his braid and plumes.
She was our only link, grandfather,
without whom we can only dip colors
and pass at a safe distance,
never able to come alongside.

Howard Moss

THE MEETING

It never occurred to me, never,
That you were attached to your universe,
Standing on a corner, waiting for a bus,
While the thought-trees grew above your head
And a meadow stretched its rambling sward
All the way up Fifth Avenue.
I was thinking of myself thinking of water,
Of how, each day I went about my job,
I missed one break in the Atlantic Ocean,
Of how I might have been here or there,
Fishing off the coast of Mexico,
Turning the sailboat round the bay,
Or, my chin resting on the concrete edge
Of a swimming pool, I could survey a hill,
The cows' soft blotches stranded in the grass.
Maybe it was that, that last green thing,
That led me into your deepening meadow,
That made me turn among the giant stones
To look one minute into your mind,
To see you running across a field,
The flowers springing up where you had touched.
It was there, I think, we finally met.

LONG ISLAND SPRINGS

Long Island springs not much went on,
Except the small plots gave their all
In weeds and good grass; the mowers mowed
Up to the half-moon gardens crammed
With anything that grew. Our colored maid

Lived downstairs in a room too small
To keep a bird in, or so she claimed;
She liked her drinks, sloe-gin, gin-and...
When she was fired, my grandma said,
"Give them a finger, they'll take your hand."

So much for the maid. My grandma lived
In a room almost as small. She gave
Bread to the birds, saved bits of string,
Paper, buttons, old shoelaces, thread...
Not peasant stock but peasant—the real thing.

What stuff we farmed in our backyard!
Horseradish that my grandma stained beet-red—
Hot rouge for fish—her cosmos plants
With feathery-fine carrot leaves, and my
Poor vegetables, no first class restaurant's

Idea of France. "Your radishes are good,"
My sister said, who wouldn't touch the soil.
My mother wouldn't either. "Dirt, that's all."
Those afternoons of bridge and mah-jongg games,
Those tournaments! Click-click went forty nails

That stopped their racket for the candy dish.
"Coffee, girls?" came floating up the stairs.
Our house was "French Provincial." Chinese mirrors
Warred against the provinces. The breakfast nook
Had a kind of style. But it wasn't ours.

I'd walk down to the bay and sit alone
And listen to the tide chew gum. There was
An airport on the other shore. Toy-like,
It blew toy moths into the air. At night,
We'd hear the distant thunder of New York.

Grandpa, forgive me. When you called for me
At school in a sudden rain or snow, I was
Ashamed that anyone would see your beard
Or hear you talk in broken English. You
Would bring a black umbrella, battle-scarred,

And walk me home beneath it through the lots,
Where seasonal wild roses took a spill
And blew their cups, and sumac bushes grew
Up from the sand, attached to secret springs,
As I was secretly attached to you.

Friday night. The Bible. The smell of soup,
Fresh bread in the oven, the mumbling from
The kitchen where my grandma said her prayers.
Reading the Bible, she kept one finger under
Every line she read. Alone, upstairs,

The timelessness of swamps came over me,
A perpetual passing of no time, it seemed,
Waiting for dinner, waiting to get up
From dinner, waiting, waiting all the time.
For what? For love, as longed-for as a trip

A shut-in never takes. It came to me.
But what Proust said is true: If you get
What you want in life, by the time you do,
You no longer want it. But that's another
Story, or stories, I should say, much too

Pointless to go into now. For what
Matters to me are those lifelong two

Transplanted figures in a suburb who
Loved me without saying, "I love you."
Grandpa, tonight, I think of you.

Envoi:
Grandma, your bones lie out in Queens.
The black funeral parlor limousines
Just make it up the narrow aisles.
When flowers on your headstone turn to moss,
Russian cossack horses leap across
The stone, the stone parentheses of years.

STARS

For James Merrill

In some versions of the universe the stars
Race through their orbits only to arrive
Back where they started from, like me planning to
Visit you in Greece—how many times?—I never have,
And so your house in Athens still remains
A distinct possibility, like one the stars
Foretell in the sky or spell out on the magic
Ouija board you use to bring to life,
Out of the night's metaphysical static,
Ephraim, that Greek, first-century Jew
Who telegraphs his witty messages to you,
The cup as pointer capturing alive
The shorthand of the occult, divinely comic . . .
But who's responsible for the result—
The spirit world or you?

          Do you as I do
Have to fend off Freud's family reunions:
Those quadraphonic old familiar quartets
Positioned nightly, bored, around the bed—
No speaking parts, and two of them at least
Certified deadheads? What does friendship mean
Unless it is unchanging, unlike Ovid's
Metamorphoses where everyone's becoming
Something else—Poor Echo and her voice!
And poor unlistening, unhinged Narcissus;
Poised above the water for the glassy foreplay,
He sees more than himself in the reflecting pool:
It's Algol, the ecliptic—a variable.
We met in the forties (hard to believe—
You were in uniform and I in mufti.—)
And went our separate ways: you to matinées
At the Opera and I to the City Ballet.
Though one extraordinary day, much later,

We heard "Wozzeck" at a dress rehearsal,
Sitting in the empty Met at 39th Street
In a center box—was it Mrs. Morgan's?
(How much more pertinent to this poem's theme
If it had belonged to Mrs. Astor!)
The nascent glitter of the oval boxes,
Brass railings sheathed in velvet, dimming lights
Preparing the round hush for music's entrance,
The subtle musk of perfumed dust, and dusky
Presences, now ghosts, floating round the room
(Now itself a ghost, long since torn down):
Old opera stars and their old audiences.
What a performance! Never interrupted
Once by—God!—was it Mitropoulos?
I think it was. Another Greek. You know
How memory fuzzes up the facts. But one
Odd fragment still remains. You brought along
A paper bag with chicken sandwiches
We ate out in the lobby in the intermissions,
And never was a sandwich so delicious—
Drunk on music, we staggered down the stairs
To daylight streaming in to air the lobby,
Surprised to see—beyond the doors—Broadway!

Loew's "Valencia"'s ceiling made of stars
Was not "The Starlight Roof"—that came later—
Starry-eyed, I watched the North Star rise
At Fire Island Pines. Below the equator,
I assumed it *fell*, and the Dipper, in reverse,
Spilled the velvet black back into darkness—
All wrong, of course. At the Planetarium,
Projected stars I craned my neck to see
Brought back the "Valencia"'s vaudeville to me,
A passion of my childhood: backbend writhers,
Lariat rope-skippers, and a stream of comic
Yodellers from Switzerland who did their stuff
Under twinkling stars. Like these above:

Calculating Leda floats above the hedges
To surprise The Swan nightly at his pool
Opal in the moonlight as he drinks his fill,
Galaxies flung at random in the till
Of the Great Cash Register the world comes down to;
When the drawer slams shut, a once and only
Big Bang Theory may be shot to hell,
And not again the great unknown designer
Fling into the firmament the shining things
Above a world grown ludicrous or tragic,
And our sick century may not recover:
The Spanish War. The Yellow Star. Vietnam.
Five . . . or is it ten by now? . . . assassinations.
The stars were crossed, the lifelines cut too soon—
And smaller fallings-off fall every day
Worse for being seen against the view
Of the starlight's inexhaustible display
Of which we cannot make out half the meaning . . .
Did Starbuck, on his watch, stare to starboard,
Gazing at the sea through meteoric showers,
And hear, above, the music of the spheres?
Or merely hear the watch bells chime the hours?

The Little Dipper in East Hampton dips
Above the pines, as if, at my fingertips,
Light so highly born could be borne down
From vibrancies that glisten and touch ground . . .
It brings the dawn, it brings the morning in.
I'm having coffee and reading your "Divine
Comedies." At "D": "*Dramatis Personae* . . .
Deren, Maya . . ." Maya and I once met
In Washington Square and talked for hours
Of images. Was film sheer poetry? Etcet.
Of "Meshes of the Afternoon," "At Land" . . .
I saw myself in both films recently . . .
How much I had forgot! My part's half cut . . .
I dazzled myself, though, just by being young.
And "Auden, Wystan," master star of all,

A major figure in the "Comedies,"
Poured wine for me at Cherry Grove and said
At least ten brilliant things too fast to hear—
Part wit, part stammer, part schoolboy pioneer,
His high-Church, camp, austere "My dear,"
Soon switched into the beach vernacular.
I've found that conversations with the great
Are almost invariably second-rate,
Yet, when he died, I felt that truth had left
The world for good, its foremost spokesman gone.
You meet the characters in Proust at parties,
Dimly aware that you are one yourself
Fated to be translated badly like
A comedy of manners curried into Greek
With too many stars, none self-effacing,
Or worse, find yourself dressed for a Fable,
Lightly disguised as the Star of Ages . . .
Saying that, I feel the slightest pull . . .
How odd! I think I'm drifting . . . Lifted up
Past houses, trees . . . And going up and up . . .
You're rising, too, into the stellar soup . . .
Stop! Where's Newton! Where is *gravity?*

In observation cars, beneath balloons,
We falter, float into the atmosphere
Of Webster's Third . . . or is it the O.E.D.?—
Either is outer space for you and me—
And soar aloft among word constellations.
The stars are verbs; the nouns are nova; pale
Adjectives grow bold at our approach;
The sulphur schools of fish are lit, and flare;
Paper fire-cinders feather into blackness
Their ember-edged remains, and then, no matter;
From your little lip of balcony you fish
Into the icy wastes; I cast my line
Into the squirming lists. Out of the blackened blue,
Racing upward into the stratosphere,
The purest draft of crystal veers toward you.

We sidle up through drop-cloths rushing down,
Go zigzag, pause, and coasting on a calm,
Reach up to pluck the stars like words to make
A line, a phrase, a stanza, a whole poem.
A planet's surface blinds us; we look down:
Moonlight's aluminum coats the molten wells...
Is that a comma? Or a quarter moon?
One decimal of saturated gold,
A coin drops in its slot, and turns to ash.
You scud into a diamond bed ahead,
I drop toward burning coals that soon grow cool...
Exclamation marks against the sky,
Our hanging baskets periods below,
We sway, like ski-lifts hung from chains. The dark
is filled with phosphorescent question marks.
In a snow shuttle, the Great Bear flies,
Angling for the Pole. How light his fur!
The Dog Star puts his solar collar on.
It's crystal-cold. One needs the inner darkness
Lit by spirit lamps or, like Aladdin's,
Rubbed to bring the genie, warmth, back home.
Stupendous flocks... Is it the world in flames?
Or just the Milky Way? Too late! Too late!
Again we rise up through the lit bazaars,
Punchdrunk, against the carbon, seeing stars.

Ruth Herschberger

POEM

Love being what it is, full of betrayals,
Rich and ripe; love being filled with trials,
Juries that slander and black ravens' breasts
That swim like swans in the night. Life being
A true well-motored pageant, the kind
That rain pours on, making the gilt run white,
Streamers hang dankly, and pure colors merge.
Love being, life being, the words
Of dissatisfied people; it is not impossible
That we should desire nature above all,
Regarding humans as somehow outside the show,
Late arrivers, mere artifacts, pure rationals,
Let them look, let them think,
Their hopes are retinal.

MULBERRY STREET

I saw the festivities in the streets
And laughed at the pope decked in garlands
Of green, the bills of parishioners,
He sat doll-like, casting still benedictions
Toward all who did not covet the grasslike cash
Which, round his averted middle, spread
In lieu of feet and persimmony shoes.
What socks of pearls had he, what garters,
Pledges of silver, coins with the faces of civil kings,
Oh he was well-founded in temporal things,
And the winter, the coming winter, provided for:
It was not likely the pope should suffer the cold,
Nor truthfully, those presidents that sat upon the shining dimes.

SUMMER MANSIONS

The blistering proof lies in the enclosed rose and the black-eyed susan.
That time should so despair of us, the cucumbers kept yellow.
Time and dishonesty rage in an innocent tribe
Over the hardened pine floor of outmoded needles.
To call it Anxiety, or those other adages,
Is not so fair as to say gentleness and warmth,
Kindness and humanity, the rapport with the clouds,
Legs treading the pedal, and the deep swim,
Coming wet-dropped out of the water
And the raft lining itself with bathers in the sun.
Is this not the image sought, in the red swing,
The impalpable unswiveling rope,
Or the underwater radar? Sandwiches and movie,
The music of ports and of calls, scruff of the neck,
Warmth and confession of goodness under the tree
Where the soft sward is interrupted by the tread of
The tread of whom, what, drunken loiterer?
But the lips and the hard bark of the tree counseled.
Persons took, and the persimmon was eaten, whole,
Luscious and frost-sweetened; new corn on the cob.
The divinity of happiness is a thing apart.
It doesn't matter whose sense it makes.
It is the kinesthesia of truth, the snap of the good muscle,
The vanish and vanquishment of the stumbling reflex.
To watch, to be spectator, but to dive also,
To climb, jump, leap, to spring at the need,
And lie in connubial tenderness thereafter.
Such are percale, athletic, the hot garden in the sun,
And the chipping sparrows with their red-notched heads.
Anyone can understand happiness; it is the universal.
The blue sky is accessible merriment to any, or we can try.

Cid Corman

BIG GRAVE CREEK

THE PIONEERS

Trees in the river
in the familiar
eternal foreground

grizzly skeletons
just toppled over
earthpacked jutting roots

green heads in the stream
putting forth new shoots,
some are sliding down

even as you watch—
it seems—and some were
drowned so long ago—

bleached arms start out from
amidst the current
to grasp at the boat

and drag it under.
Evening changes all.
Five men five women

and a little girl
emigrate ashore.
All their worldly goods

a bag, a large chest,
and one old highbacked
rushbottomed chair. Foot

of a high bank, sun
red on the water,
on the treetops fire.

Men out first and help
the women and things,
bid rowers goodbye

and shove the boat off.
At the first plash the
oldest woman sits

down in the old chair
close to the water
without a word. They

stand where they landed
as it stricken stone,
eyes upon the boat.

There they stand yet. You
can see them, through the
glass, in the distance,

increasing darkness,
mere specks: lingering.
And slowly lose them.

THE POPPY

On the narrow road
out by a cache of
rocks, clumps of grass,
clover patches,

the car had a flat.
It started raining.
Two goatherds, of no
special age,

in goatskin chaps,
vests of goathide,
strayed over
to catch the operation,

to say hello. No
more than ten minutes;
the goats not stopping
a moment.

Someone picked a poppy,
stuck it in a notch
of the hood
at the windshield.

The wiper all the way
to the coast slashed
and the wind whipped
the flower. By

the time the car
arrived only
an imaginary scarlet
stained glass.

I PROMESSI SPOSI

A schoolteacher his hair curled thin and gray bespectacled
his fiancée from a village in Puglie very young and very well put
    together

Her father a lean white-moustached small soul got up in scrubbed
    churchclothes
and tight shoes a little unnerved by the traffic

The professor his betrothed and her father stand in the square
the men's hands behind them and hers constantly at her hair

They stand of course in the sunlit square
between the Banca di Napoli San Giovanni and the stores

The future groom will introduce a few friends nod salute the many
buy his future bride and future father-in-law

coffee and cassate if they desire at La Calamita
or drink an amaro with the old man like a pledge

It is all very simple and formal a quiet event
a kind of insurance a kind of end

THREE TINY SONGS

I have come far to have found nothing
or to have found that what was found was
only to be lost, lost finally
in that absence whose trace is silence.

*   *   *   *

It is hard when you're dying to believe
anything is or could have been or will be—
death begins to dream a dream of its own.

*   *   *   *

A man dies.
That's all. The
contraction
of that *is*.

Harold Witt

WALKING MILWAUKEE

At the end of everything, I walk Milwaukee
between the elms cathedraling the blocks
and hotbox houses in the muggy weather—
over to Sherman, or drive to Brown Deer Park.
No one is there to glide the moss but ducks
and under birch and willow only us

to walk in clover, sweating as we walk
with Grandma and the babies by the pond—
who would have thought, in summer hot Milwaukee,
we'd find green vacancies at six o'clock?—
but yesterday I saw a rabbit hop,
as if through grass, across a concrete street

as I was walking, thinking as I walked,
and saw a squirrel flitting up a trunk
while fattened housewives talked among their lawns—
this One Way flatness wildly overflowing
its sober German rules and regulations—
madness of beer, preponderance of paunch.

I walk the miles of square and ugly blocks
scanning the bricks for out of place clematis—
a purple tropic climbing up a string—
drive miles to look at Wright's Greek Orthodox
crown round church, beneath whose darkblue dome,
above eye windows, thorns are waterspouts—

a far out marvel; no one would have thought
concrete could flow so rightly in a ring
except a mind in bitter anguish caught
seeing such blocks of boxed-in suffering—

SCHLITZ signs sizzle, DON'T WALK goes on and off
at this hot endless end of everything.

Past Silver Spring—the names sound meadow cool—
we walk and talk on Grandpa's clovered grave—
death of a salesman—Grandpa sold the lots—
the carving on the stone is "beautiful"—
we talk above him on Valhalla's plots,
smelling the smoke from backyard barbecues—

who will lie where when similarly boxed;
a later generation climbs the stones
over the rigid burghers locked below.
Grandma says the trees, because the roots
would crack the coffins, can't be planted close.
Whom are the plastic flowers meant to fool?

I have to walk—through smogs of Fond du Lac—
the name is lovely but the street goes on
past smoke black bricks, past churches pointing up
to nothing but a boiling murkiness—
thundering dark about to split and drop
gutterflooding water that won't help—

the lightning seems to dramatize a god
whose wise displeasure makes the hailstones bounce,
but soon it's over and I walk again
through heated green beside Menomonee River—
(along the banks, because of antique drains
polluting purity, dead fish glitter)—

and on and on, beside the dying elms
(a blight is killing them the city over)
arching a Paradise, to hear Grandma tell,
under the willows, in the parks of clover
I walk Milwaukee in the still hot weather
and think of Dante sweating through his hell.

NOTRE DAME PERFECTED BY REFLECTION

Beside the very view of Notre Dame's
rippling rose window upside down in water,
a reek of winos curls asleep on stone;
a woman dips dim clothes in nuns and spire.

Displeased at easels, artists squint through thumbs,
pondering why bridges continually recede
past a Louvre hung with painted problems,
baigneuse and saint that, bluely solved, succeed

while timid brushes blunder into green.
The fisher's wish is for a simpler fame—
to hook among the gargoyles of inversion
something sizably silver with a fin.

A tarry tug comes breaking buttresses,
shattering to abstracts the merely mirroring mind—
nuns and winos plunge through oily rainbows,
a five-eyed limpid poet splits and drowns,

the ripping lips of fish are anglers' own,
the woman washes gowns in artists' blood.
It is a matter of reflection, not perfection,
whether views are evil, true or good.

Perspective straightens in the crooked Seine
as tugs chug, dripping drapeaus, farther on,
and then the mind perfects this ecstasy,
a wavering vision entranced to glass and stone.

Anne Stevenson

AFTER HER DEATH

In the unbelievable days
when death was coming and going
in his only city,
his mind lived apart in the country
where the chairs and dishes were asleep
in familiar positions,
where the geometric faces on the wallpaper
waited without change of expression,
where the book he had meant to come back to
lay open on a bedside table,
oblivious to the deepening snow,
absorbed in its one story.

THE DEAR LADIES OF CINCINNATI

"Life is what you make it," my half-Italian
Grandmother used to say. And remembering how
Her purposely ludicrous voice pulled down the exalted
Ceilings of my great aunt's castle in Cincinnati
To gipsy proportions, I know that brave cliché
Was a legacy from her father. His western dream
Was a palace of chequered aprons. Ambition was color
And doom as he roared through four fortunes, strewing
Sheep, gold, horses and diamonds like sawdust
All over Kentucky. Before he died he squandered
His last square hundred on a silver tureen, a peacock
Big as a weathervane on its lid. Then what
Could his five chaste daughters do but divide up his maxims
And marry as well as they could?

                                        Uselessness
Was the use they made of their half raw beauty,
And they all found husbands who, liking their women gay,
Preserved them in an air-tight empire made of soap
And mattresses. There, for years, they manufactured
Their own climate, generated events to keep
Everybody laughing. Outside, the luck of Republicans
Fluctuated, stocks were uncertain. Sadness perplexed them, but
The aunts kept their chins up trying on hats,
Called everybody "sugar," remembered the words of hit tunes
They'd been courted to, avoided the contagion of thought
So successfully that the game kept time to the music
Even as the vanishing chairs put my grandmother out
And sent my sad over-dieted uncles upstairs
Trailing cigar-brown panelling into their bedrooms.
Yet the eyes in the gilded frames of their portraits have nothing
Unpleasant to say. The red wax roses are dusted
But not arranged. The vellum Catullus crumbles
Behind the glass doors of the bookcase, frail as the oakleaf
Fifty years dead in its cloudy, undulating pages.

And the ladies, the ladies still sit on the stone verandah,
In the bamboo chairs upholstered with chintz geraniums,
With the white painted wrought iron furniture still in bloom,
Laughing and rocking and talking their father's language
While the city eats and breathes for them in the distance,
And the river grows ugly in their perpetual service.

NORTH SEA OFF CARNOUSTIE

FOR JEAN RUBENS

You know it by the northern look of the shore,
by the salt-worried faces,
by an absence of trees, an abundance of lighthouses.
It's a serious ocean.

Along marram-scarred, sandbitten margins
wired roofs straggle out to where
a cold little holiday fair
has floated in and pitched itself
safely near the prairie of the golf course.
Coloured lights are sunk deep into the solid wind,
but all they've caught is a pair of lovers
and three silly boys.
Everyone else has a dog.
Or a room to get to.

The smells are of fish and of sewage and cut grass.
Oystercatchers, doubtful of habitation,
clamour "weep, weep, weep" as they fuss over
scummy black rocks the tide leaves for them.

The sea is as near as we come to another world.

But there in your stony and windswept garden
a blackbird is confirming the grip of the land.
"You, you," he murmurs, dark purple in his voice.

And now in far quarters of the horizon
lighthouses are awake, sending messages—
invitations to the landlocked,
warnings to the experienced,
but to anyone returning from the planet ocean,
candles in the windows of a safe earth.

ANNE STEVENSON / 71

THE MUDTOWER

And again, without snow, a new year.
As for fifty years, a thousand years, the air
returns the child-blue rage of the river.
Six swans rise aloud from the estuary,
ferrying tremendous souls to the pond by the playground.
They're coming for me! No. I'm a part of the scenery.
They fly low, taking no interest in migratory ladies.

The stone town stumbles downhill to untidy mudflats—
high square houses, shivering in windows, the street of shops,
the church and clocktower, school, the four worn pubs
artfully spaced between dry rows of white cottages.
Then council flats, fire station, rusty gasometer,
timber yard baying out its clean smell of pinewood.
Then grass, swings, mud. The wilted estuary.

You could say that the winter's asleep in the harbour's arm.
Two sloops with their heads on their backs are sleeping there
    peacefully.

Far out in the tide's slum, in the arm of the sand-pit,
the mudtower wades in the giving and taking water.

Its uses—if it ever had uses—have been abandoned.
The low door's a mouth. Slit eyes stab the pinnacle.
Its lovethrust is up from the mud it seems to be made of.
Surely it's alive and hibernating, Pictish and animal.
The sea birds can hear it breathing in its skin or shrine.

How those lighthouses, airing their bones on the coast,
hate the mudtower! They hold their white messages aloft
like saints bearing scriptures.

As the water withdraws, the mudtower steps out on the land.
Watch the fierce, driven, hot-looking

scuttlings of redshanks, the beaks of the oystercatchers.
Struggle and panic. Struggle and panic.
Mud's rituals resume. The priest-gulls flap to the kill.
Now high flocks of sandpipers, wings made of sunlight,
flicker as snow flickers, blown from those inland hills.

Frank O'Hara

THE DAY LADY DIED

It is 12:20 in New York a Friday
three days after Bastille day, yes
it is 1959 and I go get a shoeshine
because I will get off the 4:19 in Easthampton
at 7:15 and then go straight to dinner
and I don't know the people who will feed me

I walk up the muggy street beginning to sun
and have a hamburger and a malted and buy
an ugly NEW WORLD WRITING to see what the poets
in Ghana are doing these days
                                   I go on to the bank
and Miss Stillwagon (first name Linda I once heard)
doesn't even look up my balance for once in her life
and in the GOLDEN GRIFFIN I get a little Verlaine
for Patsy with drawings by Bonnard although I do
think of Hesiod, trans. Richmond Lattimore or
Brendan Behan's new play or *Le Balcon* or *Les Nègres*
of Genet, but I don't, I stick with Verlaine
after practically going to sleep with quandariness

and for Mike I just stroll into the PARK LANE
Liquor Store and ask for a bottle of Strega and
then I go back where I came from to 6th Avenue
and the tobacconist in the Ziegfeld Theatre and
casually ask for a carton of Gauloises and a carton
of Picayunes, and a NEW YORK POST with her face on it

and I am sweating a lot by now and thinking of
leaning on the john door in the 5 SPOT
while she whispered a song along the keyboard
to Mal Waldron and everyone and I stopped breathing

WHY I AM NOT A PAINTER

I am not a painter, I am a poet.
Why? I think I would rather be
a painter, but I am not. Well,

for instance, Mike Goldberg
is starting a painting. I drop in.
"Sit down and have a drink" he
says. I drink; we drink. I look
up. "You have SARDINES in it."
"Yes, it needed something there."
"Oh." I go and the days go by
and I drop in again. The painting
is going on, and I go, and the days
go by. I drop in. The painting is
finished. "Where's SARDINES?"
All that's left is just
letters, "It was too much," Mike says.

But me? One day I am thinking of
a color: orange. I write a line
about orange. Pretty soon it is a
whole page of words, not lines.
Then another page. There should be
so much more, not of orange, of
words, of how terrible orange is
and life. Days go by. It is even in
prose, I am a real poet. My poem
is finished and I haven't mentioned
orange yet. It's twelve poems, I call
it ORANGES. And one day in a gallery
I see Mike's painting, called SARDINES.

POEM

To James Schuyler

There I could never be a boy,
though I rode like a god when the horse reared.
At a cry from mother I fell to my knees!
there I fell, clumsy and sick and good,
though I bloomed on the back of a frightened black mare
who had leaped windily at the start of a leaf
and she never threw me.

I had a quick heart
and my thighs clutched her back.
I loved her fright, which was against me
into the air! and the diamond white of her forelock
which seemed to smart with thoughts as my heart smarted with life!
and she'd toss her head with the pain
and paw the air and champ the bit, as if I were Endymion
and she, moonlike, hated to love me.

All things are tragic
when a mother watches!
and she wishes upon herself
the random fears of a scarlet soul, as it breathes in and out
and nothing chokes, or breaks from triumph to triumph!

I knew her but I could not be a boy,
for in the billowing air I was fleet and green
riding blackly through the ethereal night
towards men's words which I gracefully understood,

and it was given to me
as the soul is given the hands
to hold the ribbons of life!
as miles streak by beneath the moon's sharp hooves
and I have mastered the speed and strength which is the armor of the
    world.

ANSWER TO VOZNESENSKY & EVTUSHENKO

We are tired of your tiresome imitations of Mayakovsky
we are tired
            of your dreary tourist ideas of our Negro selves
our selves are in far worse condition than the obviousness
of your color sense
                  your general sense of Poughkeepsie is
a gaucherie no American poet would be guilty of in Tiflis
thanks to French Impressionism
                        we do not pretend to know more
than can be known
                  how many sheets have you stained with your semen
oh Tartars, and how many
                        of your loves have you illuminated with
your heart your breath
                  as we poets of America have loved you
your countrymen, our countrymen, our lives, your lives, and
the dreary expanses of your translations
                              your idiomatic manifestos
and the strange black cock which has become ours despite your envy

we do what we feel
                  you do not even do what you must or can
I do not love you any more since Mayakovsky died and Pasternak
theirs was the death of my nostalgia for your tired ignorant race
since you insist on race
                  you shall not take my friends away from me
because they live in Harlem
                        you shall not make Mississippi into
                        Sakhalin
you came too late, a lovely talent doesn't make a ball
  I consider myself to be black and you not even part
where you see death
                  you see a dance of death
                              which is
imperialist, implies training, requires techniques

                                    FRANK O'HARA / 77

our ballet does not employ
                              you are indeed as cold as wax
as your progenitor was red, and how greatly we loved his redness
in the fullness of our own idiotic sun! what
"roaring universe" outshouts his violent triumphant sun!
     you are not even speaking
                              in a whisper
Mayakovsky's hat worn by a horse

A STEP AWAY FROM THEM

It's my lunch hour, so I go
for a walk among the hum-colored
cabs. First, down the sidewalk
where laborers feed their dirty
glistening torsos sandwiches
and Coca-Cola, with yellow helmets
on. They protect them from falling
bricks, I guess. Then onto the
avenue where skirts are flipping
above heels and blow up over
grates. The sun is hot, but the
cabs stir up the air. I look
at bargains in wristwatches. There
are cats playing in sawdust.
                              On
to Times Square, where the sign
blows smoke over my head, and higher
the waterfall pours lightly. A
Negro stands in a doorway with a
toothpick, languorously agitating.
A blonde chorus girl clicks: he
smiles and rubs his chin. Everything
suddenly honks: it is 12:40 of
a Thursday.
                Neon in daylight is a
great pleasure, as Edwin Denby would
write, as are light bulbs in daylight.
I stop for a cheeseburger at JULIET'S
CORNER. Giulietta Masina, wife of
Federico Fellini, *è bell' attrice.*
And chocolate malted. A lady in
foxes on such a day puts her poodle
in a cab.
          There are several Puerto
Ricans on the avenue today, which

makes it beautiful and warm. First
Bunny died, then John Latouche,
then Jackson Pollock. But is the
earth as full as life was full, of them?
And one has eaten and one walks,
past the magazines with nudes
and the posters for BULLFIGHT and
the Manhattan Storage Warehouse,
which they'll soon tear down. I
used to think they had the Armory
Show there.

        A glass of papaya juice
and back to work. My heart is in my
pocket, it is Poems by Pierre Reverdy.

Karen Snow

DREAM GIRL

Always lately   on the rim of
my dreams   is this little girl.
There's something wrong with her.
She's sallow   wilted   and somewhat
strange.

This waif follows me through a crowd
of wanderers. Refugees, I think they are;
they're so ravaged.
The other night she took hold of my skirt,
and without touching her, I led her to a
trough of tattered coats for a nap.

Another night she was a baby,
and I carried her, smelling her rancid scalp.
I kept searching for her mother   or some
adult   anyone   to take her off my hands.

Seven years ago, the baby I cuddled nightly
in my dreams was Aran. I'd feel his dollop
of cheek pressed to mine . . . the plastic pants
podding over my forearm. I'd even wake up
inhaling the sour splotch on my shoulder
where he'd spit up.
Some nights it was Aran the toddler in my lap,
his sandy toes cupped in my hand.

It took no psychiatrist to warn me it was
the old maternal surge dragging my firstborn
back from that freshman year at college . . .
back   back into my cove   to hug away old
hurts   rock away regrets.

Two years later, on the verge of Kyp's exit
to college, his infancy saturated my sleep.
I'd caress his back, fine-boned as fern . . .
lip his leaf-like ear.

But now that I've digested the departures,
the absences, of both sons (good riddance!)
. . . now that my frayed nerves have retreated
into my art like blue fingers into gloves . . .
who is this tag-a-long? this bad-breathed little
beggar?
I have no daughter . . . never wanted one;
in fact, would have dreaded a daughter.

Mamma, is she you?
She looks like the owl-eyed tyke
in that old creased photograph
—pinched between the raven-browed brothers—
your twin   and the older one who was to
thrash you   and rape you.
"There was sumpin wrong with Casey's mine,"
you told us, and excused him.

I never did.

    I spent my childhood stiff as a stick,
    waiting for you to follow through on threats.
    Once, as in a normal family, a child might
    ask her mother: *When are you going to visit
    Aunt Jen?*   I asked: "Mamma, when are you going
    to throw yourself in the mill pond?"
    "Haw!" you croaked. "I thought you'd forgot that."

    And you went on tainting our lives.

And now, three years after my mind has packaged
you: a length of driftwood in that conventional
coffin—

just when I've begun to snuggle down into my own
small success,
here you are   phantom limb
little tailgating tramp   your earache
burning a hole in my hip.

Upsy-daisy, Katie!
Here's a glass of milk for you
juice   crayons
braces for those jumbled teeth
a bed of your own
all right: even a diploma.

I guess I've always known it:
There will never be any laurels for me
never any rest
until I limn your life all over again,
dipped deeply into mine   softened   rinsed
sweetened   and re-dressed.

Jascha Kessler

A STILL LIFE

There was a feeling, I know,
as if you had bought some fruit
and put it on the table
where we could watch it ripen:
apples, pears, and oranges,
figs and a few bananas—
the hearts of sweetness, and flies.

Suppose I had not come home,
suppose you'd forgotten me,
or grown tired of this page
as the light began to fade?
I see you closing windows,
or pausing at the mirror—
I see you touching your lips.

It is here, you whispered, here
and nowhere else that it was;
like the music of traffic
in our terrible city
it must be known to be heard—
and yet nothing is harder
than to listen to one's self.

There is the wine in the glass,
and the long evening drinks it;
there were words we waited for,
and they changed us like our lives;
but the night needs only night—
so that, being what we are,
we turn to our beginnings.

LOOTING

It was that red moon rising
through our bitter city's fumes,
and the fires under our streets
that seethed pounding steel and stone
into a slow oily dust
on which we lived, like crystals
Condemned to breathe, I cried out

And that bright planet rising,
there, beyond our haggard roofs,
that distant evening friend
who follows like a good bitch
and keeps her clear eye on us,
wary of our promises
Condemned to touch, I took you

And later, that pale river
of cold light across the sky,
too far to carry us now—
what did we say it must be?
dead clouds, or a mist of souls
blown off by the polar winds...
Condemned to eat, I ate you

It was then our count began,
and we measured all our stars
and knew each one by its name,
marking its history down
from white light to russet flames,
and our night shrank, our night grew
Condemned to hear, I killed you

What was left? the world prostrate,
and in this furnace these bones,

glowing on their mound of ash,
all that remained of the past,
hissing, snapping like green wood,
charring our eyes, and the moon
Condemned to see, I sought you

Do you recall those hard roads,
frozen, gray as the small moon
hanging over these blank hills
where we wandered, drifting west
with those others, armed shadows,
men and women and their dogs?
Condemned to move, I came here

As our earth and sky went black
I stopped and stood, I waited,
without moon or stars or time—
no, you were not among them,
you were nothing anymore—
and our long night almost gone
and I was awake at last
Condemned to live, I speak now

Laurence Lieberman

THE OSPREY SUICIDES

> *Occasionally, an osprey locks its*
> *talons into a fish too large to*
> *handle and is pulled under to drown.*
> Roger Tory Peterson

1. Samurai: Suicides of the South

Casting from the Miami causeway
    near Key Biscayne,
      not a nibble
for hours into the sultry dawn (nor a scant gust,
    no faint wind-whiffles),
my last tackle lost to heavy current and the bottom-
        snags, I
    empty the bucket
  of live bait—squirming ten-legged shrimp—
         lean over the concrete guardrail, and stare
      into the water below. A blurred
        shadow, flashing, rises from the depths;
      distorted by its violent whirring,
the image seems oddly close to, as if
    somehow above, the surface—
      a ghostfish.
Now it hovers in one spot, halts, appears to settle
    on the surface, stationary
but for a checkered dazzle of black-and-white splotches
      blending
  with the pale gray-white
reflection of the bridge—all image!

      All's a mirroring, I think, as a soft
      rhythmic swishing overhead
        twists my neck in an abrupt upward reflex.

I'm arrested—checked and held—
by a brilliant osprey (the exact
twin of the mirrored
water-blur)
suspended on laboring wings, transfixed, as if impaled
on a fifty-foot pole.
Then he plunges headlong, leaving me staring into vacancy.
My eyes,
two arrows streaking
for the target, race his plumb-line descent.
He strikes the water—talons thrown forward
on long white legs extended
like pitchforks—the only visible prey
is his own unblurred mirror-double:

the two birds, bilaterally symmetrical,
collide, melting into
each other:
both ospreys explode in foam! The powerful wingbeats
breaking his dive
churn the surface into a wall of spray that hides all
but outermost
wingtips and beak
held aloft, head never submerged.
The wings, never folded, madly quicken,
working ferociously for lift-off,
as the bird slowly emerges from the cloak
of foam—airborne at last—
clutching a large red snapper
in his curled talons,
his burden
losing drag, approaching weightlessness, while he gains
speed and altitude.
As he straightens
into a vertical ascent,
his water-image dims and shrinks,

while a matching sky-image above, hanging
immobile like a lantern projection
   on the cloudscape, awaits his swift approach.
Grown distrustful of optic
      fakes, I blink my eyes in wonder. . . .
         I look again.
As the climbing osprey diminishes in size, his perfected
            sky-twin, unshrinking,
glides in a slow circle on extended wings. Before the lower
                  bird meets
         his soul-brother in heaven,
      the upper bird swoops down from above,
               declaring himself a piratical bald eagle.
         Trying to catch the osprey unawares,

      the eagle homes in on him
            and executes
a precision-timed swipe at the snapper. The smaller bird,
            screaming his outrage,
swerves at the last possible instant, easily dodging clear
                  without halting—
         or even appreciably
      slowing—his rate of ascension.
            The emperor of birds,
               infuriated, soars quickly above the osprey,
                  again and again, whose masterful
side-veerings always deftly elude
      the eagle dive-bomber's
            aerial thrusts
as both raptors, hurtling like runaway kites into the upper
      air,
      are finally reduced
to little more than speckled mote against the sky. The osprey,
      straining
         to lift his freightage, climbs
      slower and slower; his outleaps

grow fiercer; but at last
he drops the fish. The eagle, plummeting,
intercepts the falling carcass
just before it reaches the sea;
he glides
a few feet above sea level, flaunting his prize. Morning
trade winds arising,
I spot the osprey scanning the gusty bay
for surface game.
Following his search,
I notice a spread-winged highflier—
misidentified earlier
as obscure cloud-mirage—
now rapidly descending; he coasts

on motionless, vast, dark wings
outspread. Squinting
at the frigatebird's
unmistakable forked tail and webbed feet, I hardly notice
his side-slipping maneuvers
into position over the bald eagle. One savage pounce—
a bone-breaking
peck!—and his long
hooked beak instantly hijacks
the limp fish from the eagle's surprised claws,
old baldy bested by the man-of-war bird,
master of sky-to-sea pirates. The frigate
never alights on the water:
despite his onetime
water-strutting
webbed feet—now shrunken and held close to his body
on legs shortened
for total streamlining—he is unable to rise
from the sea
once fallen. The eagle
haltingly cruises downwind,

a dazed prince of the air drifting earthward.
The osprey keeps wending upward and outward, his
wings
a weft in the wind's shuttle,
his body lofted in broader circles
of a slowly upwinding
spiral.
He traces the periphery of an inverted cone with apex
near the bay's center,
extending his range of surface-tracking radar;
gauging
all points below
at once, he surveys a commanding
view of a great plain of water stretching
from shore to shore. Checking
himself at about one-hundred feet, he hovers—
a bombardier sighting his target—

and drops like a discharged projectile.
The shower of spray,
bubbling
higher and higher over the flapping wings, froths
like a small geyser
as the bird struggles to hoist
the payload
tugging him under.
The towering spume lowers, deflates,
when a blast of wind sucks his exposed wing
ends
.   and hurls him high over the swells
hefting a yards-long thick garfish,
violently
whipping about, bending its wiry silverflanks double upon
the talons piercing
its back. As the osprey levels off,
he coasts on a line
parallel to the surface, perhaps five

wingspans high. The strong head wind shifts
course and fades; the osprey
pivots to catch the last of the wind; wind
dying, he surges nose-upward
on strenuously heaving wingflaps,
his claws buried
in the gar's
spine, and sinking deeper, the fish jerking its tail in its
last
shimmering death throes.
I drop my eyes to the pair mirrored below, the reflected
battle-
thrashing of bird and prey
strangely altered by optical alchemy
into the amorous writhings of mating lovers,
the upper figure alternately lifting,
and being pulled down by the lower; but fol-
lowing
a peak of vigorous flailing

all motion quavers to a stillness.
Before I can lift
my eyes back
to the aerial pair, the aquatic pair has swallowed the origi-
nal
as echo drinks up sound.
The osprey, collapsing on outstretched
wings, falls
into its image, still hugging
its victim and slaughterer to its breast.

2. DDT: Suicides of the North

Bird lovers living near the Connecticut River estuary
connecting with Long Island Sound
erect cart wheels atop poles to lure survivors
of the dwindling osprey colony.

A few mating pairs
oblige, finding the wheels'
rotted hubs and spokes apt support
for the great heavy nests of sticks.
Bird-watcher's
report.
Grim news from next door eyries.
Hatchlings, down seven-eighths. Egg-layings,
normal. Offset by mysterious egg disappearances.
Chief suspect: poacher raccoons.
Ruled out by failure of raccoon-proof nesting
platforms. Females observed sitting on unhatched eggs
for seventy days, twice the normal
gestation period—still, no brood.
Months pass.
Bizarre symptoms reported.
Conjectured DDT-onset
of hastened

senility.
Or osprey insanity.
Three foreign objects turn up in one nest:
a child's rubber ball, a cracked golf ball, a rainbow-
colored, decorative glass egg;
the nest's absent matron, returning with a near-oval
bleached white sea snail shell locked in her talons,
settles down for a five-week roost
on her new miscellaneous hatchery.
Outrage!—
across the river. An all-night freak power failure,
darkening all homes along the river's
north bank.
At daybreak, the power-and-light
inspector, hunting the fault, locates an upturned
corrugated metal trash can cover
(half-fallen from the crossbars of a power pole onto short-
circuited wires) containing a nest of large sticks, three
unbroken
osprey eggs, and a puddle of rain water

that tipped the innovatory eyrie during the night's
    downpour.
                Commonly, osprey mates choose a deserted
            island for nesting sites.
One mating couple is observed migrating inland
        from an ideally hidden eyrie on a dead spruce snag,
            stranded on Great Island by storm tides,
to build a pole nest at a busy traffic intersection;
            another pair abandons an island nest for a poletop site
                beside the railroad tracks, and develop
a preternatural immunity to the clatter and roar
        of the passing express.
                            A lone, unreasonable bald eagle,
            paying an early visit from the north
country, long before the first ice floes form
        on the river, gliding high over the Great Island nesting
                territory,
            is harried from above by a daredevil
shrieking male osprey swooping again and again
        toward his heftier imposing cousin as if trying to drive
                him
            out of violated private air space—
both birds augustly silhouetted against the sky,
        hundreds of feet above all nests.
                            The eagle, making a few
            tame feints, hardly bothering to flinch
or fight back, resumes his former course of drift,
        soaring and coasting effortlessly away from the attacker.
        Moments later, the militant osprey
slowly drops on five-foot-wide extended wings
        to his oak-limb nest, bearing a two-pound gray mullet
                in both claws, with its head
half-eaten away.
                Still nibbling as he alights
            osprey-sire, sole provider for the nesting young,
                oddly withholds his catch
from three famished nurslings—ignoring their clucks

and the mother's strident screaming—and continues
          to munch
    laterally across the body and into the tail,
as if deaf to their rising chorus of squawks.

Lee Gerlach

FOR PETER

When he had chanted thus much he ceased, and I
followed after him again . . .

You were that time's resemblance, whole and one,
The manner of change, but still in such austere
And kind regard, husband, father, and son
Of more than old event—and you were here.

What shall we think, seeing so great a change
Bewilder you? That all change is undone?
Ah now, imperishably become too strange
For us to know, you are the brink of reason.

And we hold back. Looking across that space,
We see all that we were fuse and unfold
In brilliant, loose procession: faces that face
The blinding spot across abyssal cold.

And always this—gentle singing, alone,
For dancers wandering all night long
In a dim ballroom. The air turning to stone,
Glittering a farewell commotion gone wrong.

The instrument and measure lie unstrung.
Guitar and bass, cornet laid on a chair,
Promise the fraught redemption of a song,
Love's long sustaining, and wept impatience here.

THE PILOT'S WALK

We can go on a hundred years
Like this, admiring simple things
In their setting: what belongs
And what does not, as each appears:

What in the thicket hangs beside
The wild berry, an orange leaf,
And what below the olive roof,
Raw beams where dusty spiders stride.

Painted girls in the old houses
Leaning from windows on the walk.
Harsh voices. Voices that, singing, speak.
Lank horses in loose and scarred harness.

Regret in parting, confused, still.
Meeting that promises regret.
Black hair tumbling its full weight.
Night's weight tangled with the hill.

Dead men thrown in the woods all week.
Helmets and belts that catch the sun.
Vermillion pools, earthworks, wine
Left standing. Branches and birds that creak.

Like this, admiring, vision clears.
The pastoral efficiency
Of mind turns up what it can see,
And wanders on a hundred years.

THE PILOT'S DAY OF REST

All day the pigeons near the hangar door
Have spilled the mild air, limber, from their wings.
The planes drift home in pairs as if the war
Were peace itself, a way for honoring
Their gentle bickering,
Their furtive clouded dapples, and the corps.

And all day long the air has held for peace.
The rage of barking dogs beyond the field
Came dispossessed of body, endless voice.
Prelude to swarming, bees in fervor wheeled
Instinct in motion sealed.
The autumn trees stood poised for their release.

Piebald and rose, sienna, emerald, red,
The colors of the pigeons stained the ground
And gathered in the light, and the light bred
Pendants of fire that met upon the sound
Of children singing, bound
Homeward across a field where hay was spread.

The flared bell in a distant tower awoke,
Burned through the fall of air with lip and tongue,
A humble alternation. Stroke by stroke
Those parallels, unharried, coiled and clung,
Desire that we have sung.
It was the sound, all day, of those who spoke.

I could not think of anything I knew,
Not of myself, my fear, the friends who died
As only friends may die, for the full blue
Of heaven held against the world, beside
And in me loosed the tide
Of pigeons and the light in which they flew.

Marge Piercy

GRACIOUS GOODNESS

On the beach where we had been idly
telling the shell coins
cat's paw, cross-barred Venus, china cockle,
we both saw at once
the sea bird fall to the sand
and flap grotesquely.
He had taken a great barbed hook
out through the cheek and fixed
in the big wing.
He was pinned to himself to die,
a royal tern with a black crest blown back
as if he flew in his own private wind.
He felt good in my hands, not fragile
but muscular and glossy and strong,
the beak that could have split my hand
opening only to cry
as we yanked on the barbs.
We borrowed a clippers, cut and drew out the hook.
Then the royal tern took off, wavering,
lurched twice,
then acrobat returned to his element, dipped,
zoomed, and sailed out to dive for a fish.
Virtue: what a sunrise in the belly.
Why is there nothing
I have ever done with anybody
that seems to me so obviously right?

TO BE OF USE

The people I love the best
jump into work head first
without dallying in the shallows
and swim off with sure strokes almost out of sight.
They seem to become natives of that element,
the black sleek heads of seals
bouncing like half-submerged balls.

I love people who harness themselves, an ox to a heavy cart,
who pull like water buffalo, with massive patience,
who strain in the mud and the muck to move things forward,
who do what has to be done, again and again.

I want to be with people who submerge
in the task, who go into the fields to harvest
and work in a row and pass the bags along,
who stand in the line and haul in their places,
who are not parlor generals and field deserters
but move in a common rhythm
when the food must come in or the fire be put out.

The work of the world is common as mud.
Botched, it smears the hands, crumbles to dust.
But the thing worth doing well done
has a shape that satisfies, clean and evident.
Greek amphoras for wine or oil,
Hopi vases that held corn, are put in museums
but you know they were made to be used.
The pitcher cries for water to carry
and a person for work that is real.

THE ROOT CANAL

You see before you an icing of skin,
a scum of flesh
narrowly wrapped around a tooth.
This too is red as a lion's
heart and it throbs.
This tooth is hollowed out to a cave
big enough for tourists
to go through in parties with guides
in flat-bottomed boats.
This tooth sings opera all night
like a Russian basso profundo.
This tooth plays itself like an organ
in an old movie palace; it is
the chief villian, Sidney Greenstreet,
and its laughter tickles with menace.
This tooth is dying, dying
like a cruel pharaoh, like a
fat gouty old tyrant assembling
his wives and his cabinet, his horse
and his generals, his dancing girls
and his hunting cheetah, all
to be burned on his tomb
in homage. I am nothing,
nothing at all, but a reluctant
pyramid standing here, a grandiose
talking headstone for my tooth.

Nancy Willard

MOSS

A green sky underfoot:
the skin of moss
holds the footprints of
star-footed birds.

With moss-fingers, with
filigree they line
their nests in the
forks of the trees.

All around the apples
are falling, the leaves
snap, the sun moves
away from the earth.

Only the moss stays,
decently covers the
roots of things, itself
rooted in silence:

rocks coming alive
underfoot, rain no
man heard fall. Moss,
stand up for us,

the small birds and
the great sun. You know
our trees and apples,
our parrots and women's eyes.

Keep us in your green
body, laid low
and still blossoming
under the snow.

SAINTS LOSE BACK

And there was complacency in heaven
for the space of half an hour,
and God said, Let every saint lose his back.

Let their wings and epaulettes shrivel,
and for immortal flesh give them flesh of man,
and for the wind of heaven a winter on earth.

The saints roared like the devil.
O my God, cried Peter, what have you done?
And God said,

Consider the back,
the curse of backache
the humpback's prayer.

Consider how thin a shell man wears.
The locust and crab are stronger than he.
Consider the back, how a rod breaks it.

Now consider the front, adorned with eyes,
cheeks, lips, breasts, all
the gorgeous weaponry of love.

Then consider the back, good for nothing
but to fetch and carry, crouch and bear
and finally to lie down on the earth.

Oh, my angels, my exalted ones,
consider the back,
consider how the other half lives.

THE FLEA CIRCUS AT TIVOLI

Let a saint cry your praises, O delicate
desert companion, the flea.
So tiny a mover ruffles his faith
and sends him, scratching and singing,
praising the smallest acrobats of God.

The lady with alligator hips and
hummingbirds in her hair tramples invisible trumpets.
The lights in her eyes dim.
Now from an ivory box her tweezers pluck
three golden chariots and a cycle, spoked
like a spider, drumming the swath of green.

"Behold," cries the lady with delphinium voice,
"Olaf and Alfred and Madame Wu, three fleas
of ancient lineage, fed at my own breast
will race to this miniature castle of pearls."
In the twilight of her eyes, the gold
wagons advance, cautious as caterpillars.

But for the drivers, who can describe
them, save that each carriage moves?
That a golden bicycle whirls forever
toward heaven, moved by invisible hands?
"For those who doubt, here is a glass
which reveals the cause of the tiniest motions."

But clearer than any glass, we believe,
we admire their wizard beaks and their tiny legs
pumping the wheels hard, their gardens and parliaments,
pleasing as postage stamps, commemorative,
and we go out praising.

BONE POEM

The doctors, white as candles, say,
You will lose your child.
We will find out why.
We will take a photograph of your bones.

It is the seventh month of your life.
It is the month of new lambs and foals in a field.

In the X-ray room, we crouch on an iron table.
Somebody out of sight takes our picture.

In the picture, my spine rises like cinder blocks,
my bones, scratched as an old record,
my ribs shine like the keys on a flute,
have turned to asbestos, sockets and wings.

You are flying out of the picture,
dressed in the skin of a bird,

You have folded your bones like an infant umbrella,
leaving your bone-house like a shaman.

Here we are both skeletons, pure as soap.
Listen, my little shaman, to my heart.
It is a hunter, it beats a drum all day.
   Inside run rivers of blood, outside run rivers of water.
   Inside grow ships of bone, outside grow ships of steel.

The doctor puts on his headdress.
He wears a mirror to catch your soul
which roosts quietly in my ribs.
Thank God I can tell dreaming from dying.

I feel you stretching your wings.
You are flying home.
You are flying home.

WHEN THERE WERE TREES

I can remember when there were trees,
great tribes of spruces who deckled themselves in light,
beeches buckled in pewter, meeting like Quakers,
the golden birch, all cutwork satin,
courtesan of the mountains; the paper birch
trying all summer to take off its clothes
like the swaddlings of the newborn.

The hands of a sassafras blessed me.
I saw maples fanning the fire in their stars,
heard the coins of the aspens rattling like teeth,
saw cherry trees spraying fountains of light,
smelled the wine my heel pressed from ripe apples,
saw a thousand planets bobbing like bells
on the sleeve of the sycamore, chestnut, and lime.

The ancients knew that a tree is worthy of worship.
A few wise men from their tribes broke through the sky,
climbing past worlds to come and the rising moon
on the patient body of the tree of life,
and brought back the souls of the newly slain,
no bigger than apples, and dressed the tree
as one of themselves and danced.

Even the conquerors of this country
lifted their eyes and found the trees
more comely than gold; *Bright green trees,*
the whole land so green it is pleasure to look on it,
and the greatest wonder to see the diversity.
During that time, I walked among trees,
the most beautiful things I had ever seen.

Watching the shadows of trees, I made peace with mine.
Their forked darkness gave motion to morning light.
Every night the world fell to the shadows,

and every morning came home, the dogwood floating
its petals like moons on a river of air,
the oak kneeling in wood sorrel and fern,
the willow washing its hair in the stream.

And I saw how the logs from the mill floated
downstream, saw otters and turtles that rode them,
and though I heard the saws whine in the woods
I never thought men were stronger than trees.
I never thought those tribes would join their brothers,
the buffalo and the whale, the leopard, the seal, the wolf,
and the men of this country who knew how to sing them.

Nothing I ever saw washed off the sins of the world
so well as the first snow dropping on trees.
We shoveled the pond clear and skated under their branches,
our voices muffled in their huge silence.
The trees were always listening to something else.
They didn't hear the beetle with the hollow tooth
grubbing for riches, gnawing for empires, for gold.

Already the trees are a myth,
half gods, half giants in whom nobody believes.
But I am the oldest woman on earth,
and I can remember when there were trees.

X. J. Kennedy

ON A CHILD WHO LIVED ONE MINUTE

Into a world where children shriek like suns
Sundered from other suns on their arrival,
She stared, and saw the waiting shape of evil,
But couldn't take its meaning in at once,
So fresh her understanding, and so fragile.

Her first breath drew a fragrance from the air
And put it back. However hard her agile
Heart danced, however full the surgeon's satchel
Of healing stuff, a blackness tiptoed in her
And snuffed the only candle of her castle.

Oh, let us do away with elegiac
Drivel! Who can restore a thing so brittle,
So new in any jingle? Still I marvel
That, making light of mountainloads of logic,
So much could stay a moment in so little.

NUDE DESCENDING A STAIRCASE

Toe upon toe, a snowing flesh,
A gold of lemon, root and rind,
She sifts in sunlight down the stairs
With nothing on. Nor on her mind.

We spy beneath the banister
A constant thresh of thigh on thigh—
Her lips imprint the swinging air
That parts to let her parts go by.

One-woman waterfall, she wears
Her slow descent like a long cape
And pausing, on the final stair
Collects her motions into shape.

JAPANESE BEETLES

1

Imperious Muse, your arrows ever strike
When there's some urgent duty I dislike.

2

By the cold glow that lit my husband's eye
I could read what page eight had said to try.

3
To Someone Who Insisted I Look Up Someone

I rang them up while touring Timbuctoo,
Those bosom chums to whom you're known as "*Who?*"

4
Parody: Herrick

When Vestalina's thin white hand cuts cheese
The very mice go down upon their knees.

5
The Minotaur's Advice

Unravel hope, but be not by it led,
Or back outside you shall hang by a thread.

6

On his wife's stone, though small in cost and small,
Meek got a word in edgewise after all.

7
Translator

They say he knows, who renders Old High Dutch,
His own tongue only, and of it not much.

8
To a Now-type Poet

Your stoned head's least whim jotted down white-hot?
Enough confusion of my own, I've got.

9
At a Sale of Manuscript

Who deal in early drafts and casual words
Would starve the horse to death and prize his turds.

10
To a Young Poet

On solemn asses fall plush sinecures,
So keep a straight face and sit tight on yours.

IN A PROMINENT BAR IN SECAUCUS ONE DAY

To the Tune of "The Old Orange Flute"
or the Tune of "Sweet Betsy from Pike"

In a prominent bar in Secaucus one day
Rose a lady in skunk with a topheavy sway,
Raised a knobby red finger—all turned from their beer—
While with eyes bright as snowcrust she sang high and clear:

"Now who of you'd think from an eyeload of me
That I once was a lady as proud as could be?
Oh I'd never sit down by a tumbledown drunk
If it wasn't, my dears, for the high cost of junk.

"All the gents used to swear that the white of my calf
Beat the down of the swan by a length and a half.
In the kerchief of linen I caught to my nose
Ah, there never fell snot, but a little gold rose.

"I had seven gold teeth and a toothpick of gold,
My Virginia cheroot was a leaf of it rolled
And I'd light it each time with a thousand in cash—
Why the bums used to fight if I flicked them an ash.

"Once the toast of the Biltmore, the belle of the Taft,
I would drink bottle beer at the Drake, never draft,
And dine at the Astor on Salisbury steak
With a clean tablecloth for each bite I did take.

"In a car like the Roxy I'd roll to the track,
A steel-guitar trio, a bar in the back,
And the wheels made no noise, they turned over so fast,
Still it took you ten minutes to see me go past.

"When the horses bowed down to me that I might choose,
I bet on them all, for I hated to lose.

Now I'm saddled each night for my butter and eggs
And the broken threads race down the backs of my legs.

"Let you hold in mind, girls, that your beauty must pass
Like a lovely white clover that rusts with its grass.
Keep your bottoms off barstools and marry you young
Or be left—an old barrel with many a bung.

"For when time takes you out for a spin in his car
You'll be hard-pressed to stop him from going too far
And be left by the roadside, for all your good deeds,
Two toadstools for tits and a face full of weeds."

All the house raised a cheer, but the man at the bar
Made a phonecall and up pulled a red patrol car
And she blew us a kiss as they copped her away
From that prominent bar in Secaucus, N.J.

Lewis B. Horne

MOVING DAY

A gathering of things, boxed against
The walls, calls up the morning's wake—
Distress of self untended, beds unmade:
Each item—one, two, three—raw
And uncosmeticized,—arranged,
Sentenced to itself, bleak as rockslide stilled.

Things. Without a landscape each is robbed,
A flower budded up against
The sun to find in chalice walls a mirror.
Concave, convex—whatever line
Snaking into shape deploys,
Whatever shade eats out of shape, defines the thing—

Defines the thing to thing. Locked in. Locked out.
To us, amputation of
Our being, decomposition of the past.
Is air the only memory?
Things removed leave room for walls
To move, to close on the echo of our breath, to mirror

Dust and incoherent plain—if air
Is the only memory, if foot
Steps drum no signatures. Ledges of days
Erode, slide from beneath our feet,
While steps to the door deliver us
From disappearing things, from things to begin from.

MUSCAE VOLITANTES

*opacities that make their
appearance in the vision under
the form of dots, flocculi,
threads, or membranes*

They all array before my eyes—
structures bent and feathered like
a fossil, flaked like dandruff,
blanched cirrus-shadows poised and
ceaseless. Until I try to
watch them—when they dodge as though
the eye threw fire. I say: "Trick
them. Pretend indifference.
Then turn quickly." So I try
not to notice how they floss
impression—transparent, still.
They spawn while my back is turned.
Then I splash a glance their way.
Such indolent drift, a taunt
on the edge of sight, but on
the edge—always. Their movements look
like independent skill, like
syllables of separate
speech, bodies free in their own
sea—all to the edge of sight
between me and the far sky.
Still they come from my own clay,
dawn on me alone, are mine
alone in the bailiwick
of vision. We make common
cause, flakes in the eyes, bugs in
the system, thronging in the
membrane of a scuffy space.

Patricia Hooper

PSALM

It's not the sun
making the day sacred.

There have been other days,
brighter, and less holy.

There have been mornings
as clear, and with no pain

of being, no sharp joy.
And if the sun

has a transparency now,
how could you feel it

were it not for the leaves
illumined to that clarity;

the white table, the rushes
by the road, in the pond,

and the jay's body, its flash
among elms, clattering branches,

each carefully telling you
what it knows about light.

9:00

Waking up late this morning, in full sunlight,
I hear your voices already down in the kitchen,
trying to find the cereal, telling a joke
you've already told, and water faithfully running,
blessing the ceremony. Touching the cupboard,
touching the plate, or each other, we touch something
invisible, like a secret we almost remember,
which earth hints at. Quickly, I touch the blanket
as if in an ancient ritual, taking on texture
and strength from the threads that were once animal-fur.
If I woke in heaven, I'd say *wood, bread,* and your names.

OTHER LIVES

Some days a road streams back, a road you took
past someone's house: the porch propped up with boards,
the car dismantled in the yard, a door
where half-dressed children watch you with a look
you'd save for God. They're someone else's kids,
distant as someone else's needs and rent,
the life you never wanted if you tried.

Or it's a train you're riding: past a field
you catch a glimpse of someone hanging clothes,
long days you dreamed of, and she never looks.
Or it's a town where boys grow up to leave:
the two of them, still joking near a store,
stall like a sepia photograph, a scene
glimpsed in a 'forties movie that's run out.

Some nights you wake to this: in every house
on your own block, dark speaks with different names.
A door slams shut, dogs bark, your neighbor coughs,
a car drives up and leaves. The night's the same,
and yet its worlds are different, worlds apart.
You dream of rooms. You enter someone's life
some nights as though his heart beats in your heart.

Emery George

HOMAGE TO EDWARD HOPPER

In his landscapes silence is eloquent.
America means standstill: a marquee,
stark markings on a sunlit tenement,
nocturnal barber pole, a cloudlit sea.

A night café, a soundless conversation
behind a huge window of pure curved glass,
a forest road, abandoned service station.
One lonely figure near an underpass.

Clear morning, buildings. In a fourth-floor window
you see a bed, some suitcases: a widow.
Hotel: two men sit staring at a page.

Lampshades and landscapes. Sunlight; composition.
A city square speaks Sunday desolation.
An ancient land lies silent, and is sage.

SOLSTICE

When the music, warm of a summer's gleaming,
dies away, tuned with the revolving seasons, ·
when the trees, rich orchards and leaves are showing
    polychrome lesions;

when the light moves: glorious sun reflected,
colors stir bright, deeper than eyes had caught them
in the green; black earth is a source of sunlight
    deep into autumn;

when you then feel chill and the days grow weaker,
as the elm trees worship a light departing,
when the hoar frost pinches the leaves; your eyes are
    no longer smarting;

when the sky grows pale with receding mornings;
on the pool float leaves of a flagstone pavement;
white the sky; strong branches are silhouetted
    —sculptural moment—:

then that wonder, worship, and stars turn inward;
far the sun dips low on a bare horizon,
far and farther; swims as it enters, leaves its
    House of the Bison,

see that faithless star: we shall call, arrest him
at the needle point of his hour to vanish.
Now's the vertex moment to kindle new stars,
    now to replenish

festive fires, tall candles, the wine, the moment
here to light great logs and to lure our beastless
light to ice, flame. Carol the starlit sky, its
    moon is a mistress,

light for light. Hope bows and the world shall warm now;
lanterns, bright, burn solar: a vision, sparkless,
still beholding glory in winter, thinking
        minus all darkness,

islands, light-filled walls in a valley: houses
stand, lit up, cold-warm in the arms of fires,
crystals, charred logs, built on our northern earth-half.
        Earth never tires;

sunless snow drifts cannot survive the raging
days and long nights veiled in their cloud-lined mourning.
February's silver and rose shall open
        eyes to a morning

blazing gold. Months die with the cycling distance;
sun returns with light and our carols flying.
Winter can't leap clear of that infant younggreen—
        birth is its dying.

Tom Clark

THE LAKE: CODA

Last night I dreamt I saw
Your face in the lake   I hid till
With the sun the small
People in the lake awoke   And shook

The dew from their silk jackets
Aloft to flowers and grasses
Like a morning lamp, and swept
Sleep from the woods with wings

Like tiny brooms   Until the ways
Of the minor world glowed
With traffic in each inch, and day
Rung from pool to hilltop like a bell

You live with the pale and weak
And meek ones in the mud
To whom the keys of the air are given
And lights rising throne on throne

A DIFFERENCE

Something fallen out of the air, some
thing that was breathing there before
stopped: or say it is a difference

felt quickly on turning from one's work
to the window, and seeing there the same
trees the same color, the sky still without clouds,

changed only in reference to the trees
which also seem to have turned away.
The world still external but less distinct

at its center. For a few
seconds. Fall. The centerfielder drifts under
the last fly ball of the summer, and puts it away.

THE KNOT

l'homme n'est qu'un noeud de relations,
les relations comptent seules pour l'homme
                                    St-Exupéry

The four of
them together
beneath the roof
of the one
room school—

some one's
relative
is in the photograph—

in my hand
it breaks, a leaf
found in a book,

the yellow veins, the brown
split edges. I

Imagine them—the four

together—holding
hands; all are

dead now. A man
is his relations
with men, he

is strings
coming together

to form a knot,

who
has had a hand in it.

Tom McKeown

LOST IN YUCATAN

There is a face, a woman's face, coming up
Out of a green pool in Yucatan, the one
That has always been speaking, speaking
Among lush fern. This blossoming, this woman,
Who may have been waiting a thousand years,
Reaches the surface, makes no sound, locks
Her deep emerald eyes into the sun and vanishes.
There are no ripples where she parted the water.

The iguana does not stir on its branch.
The scorpion raises its tail from beneath a rock.
The stone road built by the Mayans is washed
Clean by rain. All paths to the interior
Are crowded with vines and flowers.

Everything loses its way in this place: a bird's
Call which sounds like a human voice, streams
Through the thick greens—perhaps it is a man
Seeking a woman lost centuries ago between the temple
And an altar of sacrifice, between the ocean
And the hidden quarry of the gods.

NIGHT CLOUDS

How high the night clouds that pass over us
in the great curve of sky,

drifting
toward Florida and beyond.

All birds navigating the night ride the immense
streams of air, starlight

on wings, the flow of the universe
in their gliding.

Leaves sink to the bottom of the river.
Nothing floats in this season. Triangles of moonlight

wash downstream,
imitating leaves.

The sudden dawn erases clouds and stars, the thinnest dreams.
Objects assume shape, solidity.

Now the illusions of grace must be invented once again.

THE GRAVEYARD ROAD

The brightest morning of summer,
wind blowing the leaves greener
than imagined, the lake swaying
impossibly toward the sun.

A blonde girl walks down
the graveyard road, barefoot,
ragged in her denims. Her hair
is knotted in a bun, her eyes
are radiant, reaching out.

The dead do not turn in their dark,
do not rise up, do not flow
from the grass. There is stillness
in their cool dust, like the fine
ashes of a distant planet. Part
of her is slowly turning toward
another world that no one knows.

The girl walks on, far from all
the dead or so she thinks. She pulls
a Queen Anne's lace and dreams
she sees the roots breaking stone
in their slow descent.

She looks down at her tan, thin legs,
her ample breasts; her vision of love
warms even the shaded graves.
She runs up the road, feels at that
moment, her running could unshackle
the dead, could swell her room
with yellow flowers. She thinks
this morning her eyes might flatten out
the waves, might make the lake her mirror,
a way to pass through herself and out.

The road is hot, the pebbles bite her feet.
She reaches up, loosens the ribbon about
her hair, and shakes her head, the loveliness
of her gold rains down.

Mary Baron

FOR AN EGYPTIAN BOY, DIED c. 700 B.C.

THE KELSEY MUSEUM, ANN ARBOR

It is a hollow child, delicate, frail,
A beautiful thin husk, a leather case
To keep the spirit in.
                              "The body is
A Temple of the Holy Ghost." I told
The nuns this was impossible; I see,
Here, how it's done. Shrunk down, hardened, refined,
The flesh distills into a beetle's shell,
Sacred despite disgust, protective, real.

LETTERS FOR THE NEW ENGLAND DEAD

1. Anne Bradstreet

Anne,
I think of you, the Massachusetts coast,
Your long Quarternions bound up in rhyme—
Hysteria, thrown out at empty fields.
The Earl of Lincoln ran a different house.

> *I found a new world at which my heart rose.*
> *I was convinced it was the Way of God;*
> *I submitted to it.*

2. Emily Dickinson

In Emily's Amherst, the tombstones talk.

> *This stone is meant by its color*
> *To signify the moral character . . .*

Their correspondences were absolute;
Men were so small, against New England snows.

> *I was the slightest in the house—*
> *I took the smallest room.*

Lavinia pries; your mother lives too long.
Inside the beautiful old house, you bleach
Out white.

3. Anne Bradstreet

Anne,
I know you moved against the wilderness
Slowly, feeling the weight, the children in
Your womb. The men cut down the trees. Inside,
You hacked your way in rhymes to Lincolnshire,
To England, where the way to God was clear.
In this new land He comes like the gaunt skulls
Carved on the Concord tombs, beating black wings
Above your bed until the fever breaks.

Next time, you find Him in another fear.
With humble hearts and mouths put i' the dust
Let's say He's Merciful, as well as Just.
Say it in poems that sing like the Bay Psalms,
Incantatory, desperate, write out God
And pin Him down to Mercy, on the page.

4. John Cotton I

When I think of the sweet and gracious company
That at Boston once I had
And of the long peace of a fruitful ministry
For twenty years enjoyed,
The joy that I had in all that happiness
Doth still so much refresh me,
That the grief to be cast out into a wilderness
Doth not so much distress me.

Liar. The grief that breaks to speech goes deep,
Dark as the sea waves that you crossed, coming,
At God's command, to godforsaken lands.
You must have wondered why He needed you
To sow His word over the empty fields.

5. Epilogue

The Concord dead lie cold, taut in the earth.
The winged skulls shriek: *None shall escape the wrath*
Of the King of Terrors.

Lawrence Joseph

WHEN YOU'VE BEEN HERE LONG ENOUGH

You breathe yellow smoke, you breathe lead
beside the river, talking out loud to no one.

A rat slips by you into the cold green water.
No longer, at 6 o'clock Mass, do you kneel,

body bent over and swaying, chanting,
"Mea culpa, mea culpa, mea maxima culpa,"

offering your sorrow to the Poor Souls in Purgatory,
no longer do you dream of your mother as a child

waiting for a streetcar in the snow, praying
to St Jude to cure her sister's paralyzed hand.

When the waitress argues, "What you do is
hang them, downtown, in Grand Circus Park—

that would keep them off the streets," you don't answer.
You hear about the woman who 25 years ago touched

the back of your head and said, "It's shaped
just like your daddy's." She just sat there

and watched blood spray from her cut wrist all over
her room in the La Moon Manor Hotel. You just

shake your head. You're not surprised.
Because, when you've been here long enough

no one can make you believe the Black Cat
Dream Book provides your winning number.

Heaven answers your prayers with dust and you swallow it.
Alone, early morning, on the Wyoming Crosstown bus,

you feel the need to destroy, like everyone else,
as the doors open and no one comes on.

James Paul

EVERYTHING

At the feeder, suddenly strange birds,
Banded and shining, bright as toucans.
When I finally got home, you tried
To tell me their names, but could not.
They were gone, and nowhere in the guide,
And no wonder—it was late, and these
Were night feeders, these huge and good birds.

Your face, like an accidental gift, still
Responds to some lost surprise, some birth,
As if it were a portrait too rare to store.
At times like this, it is suddenly right
Again, as if the domed movie house could call
Forth the gorgeous crowds it deserves,
Good-hearted crowds, better than the show.

And for myself? Those islands of earth
Rising far from the river in the dry fields,
Long-haired and surprised? That empty moment
When my blood is full of rock and roll?
Yes. But suppose the music on the radio related
To the land going by, like a pinwheel on the hood?
We would have to stop everything to turn it off.

FEET, A SERMON

Not quite organs, they sprout from the ankles,
Signifying the end of the legs. Even on dancers
They are knobby disruptions of a noble calf;
Looped with veins and capable of nothing delicate,
They stay in the dark, as terse as short prayers.

Stubs, we protest. Not the proper place for us
To end at all. However we humble ourselves
To hold them up, to beckon a god to grant us
Blooms, wheels, fire, wings, even long hair,
So elevated they cry out, go numb, finally faint.

Anything but conclude this way, in two batches
of sticks wrapped in lumpy batting. Bad enough
To subdivide as we go down, let alone erupt
Into a chaos of toes, so far away—admit it—
That wiggling them has always seemed a grotesque

Miracle. Let us face our lies about our feet:
They are parodies of symmetry, images of divorce;
A billion Hindus worried Krishna's golden feet
In vain. Brothers and sisters, here our words can't
Touch; here our bodies assume the plane of the earth.

THIS TOWN

Behind the leaves of redbud and sycamore, dangling
Like pelts in the wet heat, behind the creepers,
The mobile home "New Moon" snuggles its quarter-lot.
The brown wasps fizz under the loaded raingutters;
A woman works her impossible chrysanthemums again.
The cicadas crank up in the heat, the jays clatter,
A cardinal raps its tiny tamborine, and out past
The back lots, the highway rushes into town.
This place seems eager to take the blame for things,
For what its drifting citizens have lost or stolen,
And, dreaming of better towns, we are eager to give.
Down fifty-one, the kids are drunk again. The road
Shrugs its bars, franchise places. In the hills
Beyond them, the pig farmers are ready for the kingdom.

HONEYSUCKLE

The way the earth stops at the wall,
You might think all houses anchored
In the bedrock, cut into granite, but
The dirt dives beneath the frame. The soil
Full of old moisture, holds up the house.
The house settles into the dirt, stuck there
Like an old stone half sunk in the ground,
Or the leaning, unstrung post of a fence.

By July, the honeysuckle has swarmed
Over the chainlink fence, a fat,
Fragrant animal asleep in the yard,
Drooping in the wet heat and the wasps.
The tendrils wrap the clouded metal,
Like nerves on the spinal cord; the squares
Fill with leaf. From the yellow-white
Blooms, you could pull another cord,
White, shining with the nectar in the blossom.

Then the music on the radio sometimes falls
Away like that, diffusing like a handful
Of thrown sand, shaping a ragged silence.
The string in the signal is pulled free
And the sounds, like beads, disperse,
And we keep singing; the song, in a studio
Across town, in our throats, goes on.

Peter Serchuk

WHAT THE ANIMALS SAID

*"Aspen, Colo. (AP) The frozen body of a young woman,
discovered near here Monday, has been positively
identified as that of a registered nurse from Michigan. . . .
the cause of death has not yet been determined. . . . the
body had been 'chewed by animals' and appeared to have
been moved from its original location 'probably by animals,'
the sheriff said."*

1

She was not so sweet as you would think.
Not in the damp of her hair, not in the joint of her bones.
This you can believe:
So far beyond sleep, legs spread in the cold,
A stench so foul rose up from her flesh neither
Wolf nor bear had dared to touch her.
The blue eyes and soft feet were not what you remember.
It's better to forget.
The air itself had recoiled from her blood.

2

*What brought her here we can't say,
Though perhaps kindness. She carried no weapon.
Also, she was not alone.
They walked together, in whispers, their feet
Packing the wet snow into small cakes.
His steps were large and his voice deeper.
We followed their feet past alder trees,
Past the blackberry stems which are so sweet in summer,
We followed them down to a clearing
And hid in the brush. They spoke louder,
She walked more quickly. He walked faster and grabbed
Her arm. She twisted away. He caught her again*

Holding her waist. His hands were thick and his knuckles
White as snow. She screamed, we became frightened.
She screamed, we clawed at the ice. She screamed,
We raced away towards the deep woods.
We heard her screams trail off like a gun shot.

3

You must believe he loved her.
He loved her more than love, more than pain,
The facts speak for themselves.
He had been so lonely, so terribly lonely, and you too
Know what loneliness will do to desire, and what desire does to love.
You too have wanted her.
His loneliness ached him beyond all need. Her body breathed
In the space of her clothes. He touched her
And the smell of pine rushed through his nose like fire.
He wanted her but she refused. It had been too long.
He touched her face. She screamed.
He kissed her neck. She screamed.
It had been too long. He wanted her but she refused.
He never wished her harm.
The facts speak for themselves,
He only wanted her as you.

4

It was quiet for a long time.
The light turned twice and it had snowed again.
We were hungry. It is hard to hunt in snow
And the wolverine is fast on ice. We were hungry and still
She was there. We could smell her blood push through the air
Above the trees. The air was sick. We could barely sniff the pines.
We scratched a path across the woods another time but
It was different than before. She was alone and didn't move.
Also, her clothes were gone and her blue skin stiff. She didn't twitch
When we jabbed her thigh. We took small bites.
Her flesh was tough and hard to chew. We took small bites.

We pulled her back into the thick and turned to go.
The wind was cold against our fur. We were hungry,
But the air was sick.

5

It was a hunter who finally found her.
Searching for bears he'd had no luck. He vomited twice
Behind a bush and dropped his gun. Later, they gathered
Her up into a bag for the walk back home.
"The most disgusting thing I've ever seen," one policeman said.
"You could stick your fingers clear through her cheeks."
The animals slept throughout the day,
Each in its own familiar place.

6

Tell us what repulses you, dear Human.
Tell us what frightens your children in their sleep.
Is it the rough claws and coarse teeth? Tell them
To stop crying in their beds. We are only a nightmare.
Their soft feet and tender eyes are safe.
We are not human.

7

Whoever here would die for love, let them pray
To die so blessed. I can't waste tears on her facelessness,
I can only mourn the kindness which she never knew.
She knew only our kindness, the hunter's kindness.
If whole now, she might tell us how it is to be a part
Of necessity; how the holy take sparingly, and how
The final test of love is not in the giving but the taking.
Be gentle with her bones. She has only now learned
The comfort of a hundred toes touching. The animals
Are running through the woods listening.
Let us bury her alongside all other lovers.

Garrett Hongo

WHO AMONG YOU KNOWS THE ESSENCE OF GARLIC?

Can your foreigner's nose smell mullets
roasting in a glaze of brown bean paste
and sprinkled with the novas of sea salt?

Can you hear my grandmother
chant the mushroom's sutra?

Can you hear the papayas crying
as they bleed in the porcelain plates?

I'm telling you that the bamboo
slips the long pliant shoots
of its myriad soft tongues
into your mouth that is full of oranges.

I'm saying that the silver waterfalls
of bean threads will burst in hot oil
and stain your lips like zinc.

The marbled skin of the blue mackerel
works good for men. The purple oils
from its flesh perfume the tongues of women.

If you swallow them whole, the rice cakes
soaking in a broth of coconut milk and brown sugar
will never leave the bottom of your stomach.

Flukes of giant black mushrooms
leap from their murky tubs
and strangle the toes of young carrots.

Broiling chickens ooze grease,
yellow tears of fat collect
and spatter in the smoking pans.

Soft ripe pears, blushing
on the kitchen windowsill,
kneel like plump women
taking a long, luxurious shampoo,
and invite you to bite their hips.

Why not grab basketfuls of steaming noodles,
lush and slick as the hair of a fine lady,
and squeeze?

The shrimps, big as Portuguese thumbs,
stew among cut guavas, red onions,
ginger root, and rosemary in lemon juice,
the palm oil bubbling to the top,
breaking through the layers and layers
of shredded coconut and melted cheese.

Who among you knows the essence
of garlic and black lotus root,
of red and green peppers sizzling
among squads of oysters in the skillet,
of crushed ginger, fresh green onions,
and pale blue rice wine simmering
in the stomach of a big red fish?

YELLOW LIGHT

One arm hooked around the frayed strap
of a tarblack patent leather purse,
the other cradling something for dinner:
fresh bunches of spinach from a J-Town *yaoya*,
sides of split Spanish mackerel from Alviso's,
maybe a loaf of Langendorf; she steps
off the hissing bus at Olympic and Fig,
begins the three-block climb up the hill,
passing gangs of schoolboys playing war,
Japs against Japs, Chicanas chalking sidewalks
with the holy double-yoked crosses of hopscotch,
and the Korean grocer's wife out for a stroll
around this neighborhood of Hawaiian apartments
just starting to steam with cooking
and the anger of young couples coming home
from work, yelling at kids, flicking on
TV sets for the Monday Night Fights.

If it were May, hydrangeas and jacaranda
flowers in the streetside trees would be
blooming through the smog of late spring.
Wisteria in Masuda's front yard would be
shaking out the long tresses of its purple hair.
Maybe mosquitos, moths, a few orange butterflies
settling on the lattice of monkeyflowers
tangled in chain-link fences by the trash.

But this is October, and Los Angeles
seethes like a billboard under twilight.

From used car lots and the movie houses uptown,
long silver sticks of light probe the sky.
From the Miracle Mile, whole freeways away,
a brilliant fluorescence breaks out
and makes war with the dim squares

of yellow kitchenlight winking on
in all the sidestreets of the Barrio.

She climbs up the two flights of flagstone
stairs to 201-B, the spikes of her high heels
clicking like kitchenknives on a cutting board,
props the groceries against the door,
fishes through memo pads, a compact,
empty packs of chewing gum, and finds her keys.

The moon then, cruising from behind
a screen of eucalyptus across the street,
covers everything, everything in sight,
in a heavy light like yellow onions.

ON THE ROAD TO PARADISE

Distances don't matter,
nor the roll of the road past walnut groves.
It's sky that counts,
the color of it at dawn or sunset,
a match more true to the peach
than a mix of oils by Matisse.
Or maybe it's actually weather
we love most, the way it shifts
and scatters over the state
like radio waves bouncing off the face of the moon.
The one over there, near Yuba City,
rising over a backyard garden
of onions, tomatoes, squash, and corn.
The one with the spider
scrambling through celery,
harvesting moths and mayflies
from the web it has strung between stalks.
Sometimes I wish I could harvest the weather,
reap it like wheat or rice,
store it in a silo
announcing STEADY RAIN or CLEAR SKIES on its side.
When the prices rise,
I could ship hailstorms or Santanas in orange crates,
make Safeway go broke,
do something politically efficacious for a change.
But all I really do besides writing these poems
is allow my mind to wander while I drive.
There it goes, down the arroyo,
through manzanita and Mormon tea.
Or there, up the mustard and Indian pipe on the hill.
Might as well let it.
Nothing but God and Country on the radio now.
Wolfman Jack's syndicated and the Dodgers
haven't made it to Vero Beach.
I wish this road would turn or bend,

intersect with a spy movie, some Spanish galleon,
or maybe a Chinese poem with landscapes
in brocade, mist, wine, and moonlight.
This California moon is yellow most of the time,
like it was stained with nicotine
or sealed in amber like an insect.
Why is it always better somewhere else?
Why do I always wish I was Tu Fu?

Notes on the Poets

MARY BARON (1944, Hopwood Award 1970) was born in Rhode Island and has lived most of her life on the East coast. She holds advanced degrees from the University of Michigan and the University of Illinois. Presently, she teaches English at the University of Alaska, Fairbanks, some seventy miles south of the Arctic Circle. Her first book of poems, *Letters for the New England Dead*, was published in 1974; *Wheat among bones*, her second book, came out in 1979.

JOHN MALCOLM BRINNIN (1916, Hopwood Award 1939) was born Halifax, Nova Scotia. When he was four his family moved to Detroit where he was educated by Dominican nuns and Jesuit priests. He spent a year at Wayne State University before transfering to the University of Michigan. He then did graduate work at Harvard University, taught for five years at Vassar College, and became director of the Poetry Center in New York City in 1949. In 1961, Mr. Brinnin joined the faculty at Boston University, and is now professor emeritus there. Among the honors he has received are the Levinson Prize and a grant from the National Institute of Arts and Letters. His works range from poetry, *Selected Poems* (1963) and *Skin Diving in the Virgins* (1970), to memoir, *Dylan Thomas in America* (1955), to social history, *The Sway of the Grand Saloon* (1971). He spends winters in Saint Thomas and summers in Venice.

E. G. BURROWS (1917, Hopwood Award 1940) was born in Texas, grew up in New England, and has spent most of his professional life in the Midwest. He has been manager and executive producer for the University of Michigan radio stations in Ann Arbor for many years, and has directed the National Center for Audio Experimentation in Madison, Wisconsin. His poems have appeared in numerous literary journals, including the *Paris Review*, *American Poetry Review*, the *Michigan Quarterly Review*, and *Epoch*. Five collections of his poetry and one verse drama have been published, among them: *The Arctic Tern* (1957), *Man Fishing* (1969), and *Kiva* (1976).

JOHN CIARDI (1916, Hopwood Award 1939), poet, translator, scholar, and editor, was educated at Bates College, Tufts University, and the University of Michigan. He has taught at the University of Kansas,

Harvard University, and Rutgers College, and has served as director of the Bread Loaf Writers' Conference and as poetry editor of the *Saturday Review*. Since 1940, when *Homeward to America* appeared, Mr. Ciardi has published more than a dozen collections of poems, including *This Strangest Everything* (1966), *Lives of X* (1971) and most recently *For Instance* (1979). He has also translated *The Divine Comedy* (1954, 1961, 1970) and written several children's books. He divides the year between Metuchen, New Jersey, and Key West, Florida.

TOM CLARK (1941, Hopwood Award 1963) grew up in Chicago and studied at the University of Michigan, Cambridge University (on a Fulbright), and the University of Essex. For ten years he was poetry editor of the *Paris Review*. After traveling in Europe and North Africa, Mr. Clark settled first in northern California and then in the Colorado Rockies. Among his many collections of poetry are *Stones* (1969), *Smack* (1972), and *When Things Get Tough on Easy Street* (1978). He has also written three novels, four books on baseball, and a study of Damon Runyon.

CID CORMAN (1924, Hopwood Award 1947) was educated at Boston Latin School, Tufts University, the University of Michigan, the University of North Carolina, and the Sorbonne. Since 1951, he has been the editor of *Origin* and the Origin Press. He has lived outside the United States for many years, in Japan, France, and Italy. Of the more than forty books of poetry he has written, three are *Sun Rock Man* (1962), *& Without End* (1968), and *Living/Dying* (1970). A prolific translator, Mr. Corman has done versions of Basho (*Cool Melon*, 1959, and *Back Roads to Far Towns*, 1967), Francis Ponge (*Things*, 1971), and Rene Char (*Leaves of Hypnos*, 1973). He is now living again in Boston.

DOROTHY DONNELLY (1903, Hopwood Award 1931) was born in Detroit and earned two degrees at the University of Michigan. In the 1930s, her prose sketches appeared in five numbers of Eugene Jolas's international magazine of the arts, *transition*. In 1957, she won the Harriet Monroe Award and the Longview Foundation Award. She has published poems in the *Hudson Review*, the *Michigan Quarterly Review*, the *New Yorker*, the *New Republic*, and *Poetry*. Her books are: *Trio in a Mirror* (1960), *Houses* (1970), and *Kudzu* (1979).

KIMON FRIAR (1911, Hopwood Award 1939), born on an island in the Sea of Marmora, was brought to the United States at the age of three.

Since then he has kept moving, studying at the universities of Wisconsin, Michigan, Yale, and Iowa, and teaching at the University of Iowa, Adelphi College, Amherst College, the University of California at Berkeley, the University of Illinois, and Indiana University. For five years he directed the Poetry Center in New York City. Twice he was honored by the Athens Academy for his translations, and he has also been the recipient of a Ford Foundation grant. Among his books are *Modern Poetry: American and British* (with John Malcolm Brinnin, 1951), *The Sovereign Sun, Selected Poems by Odysseus Elytis* (1974), and *Scripture of the Blind, Poems by Yannis Ritsos* (1979). He is perhaps best known for his rendering of Nikos Kazantzakis's *The Odyssey: A Modern Sequel* (1958).

EMERY GEORGE (1933, Hopwood Award 1960) teaches German and comparative literature at the University of Michigan, and is also on the staff there of the Center for Russian and East European Studies. He has written or edited nine books, including four of poetry: *Mountainwild* (1974), *Black Jesus* (1974), *A Gift of Nerve* (1978), and *Kate's Death* (1980). His latest book is an annotated translation of the complete poems of Miklos Radnoti. Mr. George's poems, translations, and reviews have appeared in numerous periodicals. He is at present editing an anthology of East European poetry with Joseph Brodsky.

LEE GERLACH (1920, Hopwood Award 1955) is chairman of the English department at the University of San Diego. He has also taught literature and writing at Stanford University, Swarthmore College, the University of Michigan, the California State Universities at San Francisco and San Diego, and the University of California at Santa Barbara. As a writing fellow at Stanford, he studied with Yvor Winters and Wallace Stegner, and he has won a number of other awards for his poems. In recent years, Mr. Gerlach has worked at rendering poems by T'ang dynasty poets, Tu Fu and Han Yu. His poems have appeared in *Poetry*, the *Paris Review*, the *Southern Review*, *Epoch*, and *Spectrum*.

BAXTER HATHAWAY (1909, Hopwood Award 1936) grew up in Kalamazoo, where he briefly held the Michigan high school pole vault record, and where he attended Kalamazoo College. His Hopwood novel, *The Stubborn Way*, was published in 1937 by Macmillan Press. After teaching at the University of Michigan, the University of Montana, and the University of Wisconsin, he moved to Cornell University to develop a writing program, which he directed for thirty years. Mr. Hathaway has written scholarly works on the history of literary criticism and in grammatical theory. As editor of *Epoch*, which he founded in 1947 and edited until 1976, he printed the poems of many Hopwood winners.

ROBERT HAYDEN (1913–80, Hopwood Award 1938) had been professor of English at the University of Michigan for eleven years at the time of his death. He was a native of Michigan, born in Detroit and educated at Wayne State University and the University of Michigan. From 1946 to 1968, he taught at Fisk University in Nashville. Among the many honors bestowed on him were the World Festival of the Arts Prize, Dakar, 1966, and the Russell Loines Award, 1970. He was twice named consultant to the Library of Congress, and his volume *American Journal* was nominated for the National Book Award in 1978. His other books include *Heartshape in the Dust* (1940), *A Ballad of Remembrance* (1962), *Selected Poems* (1966), *Words in the Mourning Time* (1970), and *Angle of Ascent* (1975).

RUTH HERSCHBERGER (1917, Hopwood Award 1941) studied at the University of Chicago, Black Mountain College, and the New School for Social Research. Her Hopwood Award was in the category of Summer Poetry. She is the author of three plays, one for radio, *Edgar Allen Poe*, and two in verse, *A Ferocious Incident* and *Andrew Jackson*. The recipient of the Harriet Monroe Memorial Prize in 1953, she has written three books: *A Way of Happening* (1948), *Adam's Rib* (1948), and *Nature and Love Poems* (1969).

GARRETT HONGO (1951, Hopwood Award 1975) is a Yonsei (fourth-generation Japanese-American), born in Hilo, Hawaii, and raised in Gardena, California. He was educated at Pomona College, the University of Michigan, and Shokokuji Monastery in Japan, where he was sojourning for a year as a Thomas J. Watson Fellow. Formerly an instructor of Asian American literature at the University of Washington, and poet-in-residence at the Seattle Arts Council and the Orme School in Arizona, he is now finishing an M.F.A. in creative writing at the University of California at Irvine. His poems have been published in the *New Yorker*, *Antaeus*, and in *The Buddha Bandits Down Highway 99* (1978).

PATRICIA HOOPER (1941, Hopwood Award 1963) was born in Saginaw, and received three Hopwood Awards while at the University of Michigan. Her poems have appeared in the *American Scholar*, *Poetry*, *New Directions Anthology*, the *Chicago Review*, the *Quarterly Review of Literature*, the *Ohio Review*, *Prairie Schooner*, and *Epoch*. For several years she taught at Wayne State University and now lives in Birmingham, Michigan.

LEWIS B. HORNE (1932, Hopwood Award 1960) won his Hopwood Award in Major Fiction. He was born in Mesa, Arizona, and received his undergraduate education at Arizona State University. He has published poems in the *Fiddlehead*, the *Georgia Review, Wascana Review*, and in others, and short stories in the *Literary Review, Prairie Schooner*, and the *Best American Short Stories 1974*. He teaches in the English department at the University of Saskatchewan.

LAWRENCE JOSEPH (1948, Hopwood Award 1970) was brought up in Detroit, and studied poetry with Donald Hall at the University of Michigan. From 1970 to 1972 he did graduate studies in English at Magdalene College, Cambridge, under a fellowship from the Power Foundation, before returning to Michigan to study law. He has published poems in *Stand, Ontario Review, Broadsheet*, and other magazines. Married to the painter Nancy Van Goethem, Mr. Joseph teaches law at the University of Detroit, and has completed his first collection of poems, *Shouting at No one*.

X. J. KENNEDY (1929, Hopwood Award 1959) became a teaching fellow at the University of Michigan in 1956 and left in 1962 without a degree, "amicably." His first book of poems, *Nude Descending A Staircase* (1961), grew out of his Hopwood manuscript and received the Lamont Award. Two later collections have followed, also a book of songs, *Three Tenors, One Vehicle* (with James Camp and Keith Waldrop), an English selected poems, *Breaking & Entering* (1971), *Literature* (second edition, 1979), and other textbooks. Mr. Kennedy has held a Guggenheim fellowship and the Bruern fellowship in American civilization at Leeds University. He was professor of English at Tufts University until 1979 when he resigned in order to write. With his wife, former Michigan graduate student Dorothy Mintzlaff and five children, he now lives in Bedford, Massachusetts.

JASCHA KESSLER (1929, Hopwood Award 1952) grew up in New York, going to the University of Michigan for graduate work in 1950. Since 1961 he has been teaching at UCLA. He has had several fellowships from the Creative Arts Institute of the University of California, and went to Italy as a Fulbright scholar in 1963. In 1974, he was an NEA fellow in writing. He has published three books of poems, *Whatever Love Declares*

(1969), *After the Armies Have Passed* (1970), and *In Memory of the Future* (1976), a novel, *Rapid Transit* (1979), and two volumes of short stories, *An Egyptian Bondage* (1967) and *Death Comes for the Behaviorist* (1979). His translation of a volume of stories from the Hungarian of Geza Csath, *The Magician's Garden* (1978), won a Translation Award from the Translation Center. He has recently completed a large volume of what he calls fictive poems, or mythologems, called *Courtly Love*, which have been appearing individually in this country and abroad.

LAURENCE LIEBERMAN (1935, Hopwood Award 1952) left medical school in the fall of 1956 to start work in earnest on a first manuscript of poems. In 1964, he was hired to teach English at the College of the Virgin Islands in Saint Thomas, and his first two books of poems, *The Unblinding* (1968) and *The Osprey Suicides* (1973), dealt principally with the four years he spent in the islands. Since 1968, he has been teaching poetry workshops at the University of Illinois. In 1971, he was awarded a grant from the Center for Advanced Studies, and spent the year traveling in Japan. His collection of reviews, *Unassigned Frequencies*, appeared in 1977. *God's Measurements* (1980) is his latest book of poetry.

TOM MCKEOWN (1937, Hopwood Award 1968) has worked for the poets-in-the-schools program in Kansas, Missouri, and Michigan, and has had residence grants at Yaddo, Wurlitzer, and Ossabaw. He has traveled extensively outside the United States, visiting the Soviet Union in 1979 and 1980. He has published four volumes of poetry: *The Luminous Revolver* (1974), *Driving to New Mexico* (1974), *The House of Water* (1974), *Certain Minutes* (1978), and seven chapbooks. His poems have appeared in the *New Yorker*, the *Atlantic Monthly*, *Harper's*, *Saturday Review*, the *Nation*, and others. A cycle of his peoms, *Circle of the Eye*, was performed at Carnegie Hall, April 2, 1979.

HOWARD MOSS (1922, Hopwood Award 1940) is poetry editor of the *New Yorker*. He has received awards for his work from *Poetry* (Chicago), the National Institute of Arts and Letters, and the Ingram Merrill Foundation. In 1971 he won the National Book Award for his *Selected Poems*. Three of his plays have been produced: *The Folding Green* (1954), *The Oedipus Mah-Jongg Scandal* (1968), and *The Palace at 4 A.M. The Magic Lantern of Marcel Proust* is a critical study. Among his nine volumes of poetry are *The Toy Fair* (1954), *Second Nature* (1968), *Buried City* (1975), and *Notes from the Castle* (1979). He has edited several volumes, including *Keats* (1952) and *The Poet's Story* (1973).

FRANK O'HARA (1926–66, Hopwood Award 1951) studied music and English at Harvard University before coming to the University of Michigan for his graduate studies. Associated with the New York art world for most of his adult life, he wrote reviews and articles for *Art News* and organized exhibitions and wrote catalogues for the Museum of Modern Art. *Jackson Pollock* was published in 1959; *The New Spanish Painting and Sculpture* in 1960. His collections of poetry include *A City Winter, and Other Poems* (1952), *Meditations in an Emergency* (1957), and *Lunch Poems* (1967). In 1971, Knopf published *The Collected Poems of Frank O'Hara.*

JAMES PAUL (1950, Hopwood Award 1973) is a native of northern California. At age six he moved to northern Virginia and later studied at the State University of New York at Buffalo and the University of Michigan. He is now an assistant professor at Southern Illinois University at Carbondale, where he teaches creative writing and medieval English literature. His poems have appeared in the *American Scholar*, the *Paris Review*, *Poetry*, the *New Republic*, the *New Yorker*, and other magazines.

MARGE PIERCY (1936, Hopwood Award 1957) was born in Detroit, attended Northwestern University as well as the University of Michigan. After living in seven cities, has put down roots in Wellfleet on Cape Cod. She lives there most of the time, spends a couple of days a week in Boston, and travels often giving readings and workshops. She has published six novels, including *Small Changes* (1973), *The High Cost of Living* (1978), and *Vida* (1980). Of her seven collections of poetry, the most recent are *Living in the Open* (1976), *The Twelve-Spoked Wheel Flashing* (1978), and *The Moon Is Always Female* (1980).

NORMAN ROSTEN (1914, Hopwood Award 1938) published his *Selected Poems* in 1979. His plays, produced both on and off Broadway, include *Mister Johnson* (based upon the novel by Joyce Cary) and *Come Slowly, Eden*. A former Guggenheim fellow and recipient of an award from the American Academy of Arts and Letters, Mr. Rosten has read his work on radio and television, and "Camera Three" (CBS) has devoted a program to his poetry. His articles and reviews have appeared in *Holiday*,

McCalls, and elsewhere, and he has written two novels, *Under the Boardwalk* and *Over and Out*, and one nonfiction book, *Marilyn: An Untold Story*.

PETER SERCHUK (1952, Hopwood Award 1974) was born and raised in New York City. He attended the University of Illinois before coming to the University of Michigan for a master's degree. His poems and reviews have appeared in the *Hudson Review*, the *Paris Review*, *Epoch*, the *New England Review*, and elsewhere. Mr. Serchuk works for a large advertising agency in Detroit.

KAREN SNOW (1923. Hopwood Award 1951) is the pseudonym for a woman who won two Major Hopwood Awards. In 1978, she was awarded the Walt Whitman Prize for her book of poems, *Wonders*. She has also published short stories and one novel, *Willo* (1976). Her poems have appeared in the *Michigan Quarterly Review* and other periodicals, but largely in the *Beloit Poetry Journal*, which she calls "home." She and her husband live on an island in Puget Sound.

ANNE STEVENSON (1933, Hopwood Award 1950) is the daughter of the Michigan philosopher, C. L. Stevenson. Educated in Ann Arbor at the University High School as well as the University of Michigan, she later settled in Great Britain where she has lived and taught in Cambridge, London, Glasgow, Dundee, and Oxford. Her five books of poems include *Correspondences* (1974), a long poem in letters, *Reversals* (1969), *Travelling Behind Glass* (1974), and *Enough of Green* (1977). She has been poetry reviewer for the *Listener*, and a regular contributor to the *Times Literary Supplement* and other periodicals in Britain and America. Ms. Stevenson is editor of the magazine *Other Poetry*, foreign editor of the *New England Review*, and co-owner of the Poetry Bookshop, Hay-on-Wye, on the Welsh border, where she has also established a small publishing business.

CHAD WALSH (1914, Hopwood Award 1939) won a Hopwood Award in playwriting, but subsequently concentrated on poetry. Recently retired from Beloit College, where he taught for thirty-two years, he has also served as Fulbright lecturer in Finland and Rome, and as visiting professor at Wellesley, Juniata, Calvin, and Roanoke colleges. Among the twenty-four books Mr. Walsh has published are six volumes of verse, the latest being *Hang Me Up My Begging Bowl* (1974). A part-time Episcopal priest, he has written several works dealing with religion, such as

God at Large (1960), and the first book-length discussion of dystopian fiction, *From Utopia to Nightmare* (1962). *The Literary Legacy of C. S. Lewis* (1979) is his newest book.

NANCY WILLARD (1936, Hopwood Award 1958), the winner of five Hopwood Awards, lives in Poughkeepsie, New York, with her husband, Eric Lindbloom, himself a Hopwood winner. In 1959, she held a Woodrow Wilson Fellowship at Stanford University, and in 1967 she won the Devins Memorial Award. She teaches in the English department at Vassar College, and is a regular at the Bread Loaf Writers' Conference. The author of ten books for children and two collections of short stories, her books of poetry include *In His Country* (1966), *Skin of Grace* (1967), *Nineteen Masks for the Naked Poet* (1971), and *Carpenter of the Sun* (1974). She has also written a study of Williams, Neruda, Ponge, and Rilke entitled *Testimony of the Invisible Man.*

HAROLD WITT (1923, Hopwood Award 1947) is a coeditor of the triquarterly poetry magazine, *Blue Unicorn,* and a consulting editor to *Poet Lore.* The winner of the James D. Phelan Award for narrative poetry, a San Francisco Poetry Center Award for poetic drama, and the Poetry Society of America's Emily Dickinson Award, he has published *Beasts in Clothes* (1961), *Now, Swim* (1974), *Surprised by Others at Fort Cronkhite* (1975), and *Winesburg by the Sea* (1979). His work has been included in numerous anthologies, among them the *New Yorker Book of Poems* and *Traveling America with Today's Poets.* He is married, the father of three children, and lives in Orinda, California.

Notes on the Editors

STEVEN LAVINE (1947) teaches eighteenth-century English and twentieth-century American literature at the University of Michigan. He has published articles and reviews in *Studies in American-Jewish Literature*, *Modern Philology*, *Eighteenth-Century Studies*, and the *Michigan Quarterly Review*, and has recently completed a study entitled *The Art of the Familiar: Method and Metaphysics in Eighteenth-Century Poetry*. A member of the Hopwood Committee, he coordinated the Fiftieth Anniversary Hopwood Festival, celebrating the fifteenth anniversary of the Hopwood Awards.

HARRY THOMAS (1952), who won his Hopwood in Major Poetry in 1979, has degrees from the University of San Diego and the University of Michigan. He has taught at both these schools and as poet-in-residence at Kalamazoo College and the Orme School in Arizona. His poems, translations, and reviews have appeared in the *Southern Review*, the *Sewanee Review*, the *Michigan Quarterly Review*, and elsewhere.